D1571526

Medicolegal Issues for Radiographers

Medicolegal Issues for Radiographers

3rd Edition

Robert J. Parelli, M.A., RT(R)

S^t_L

ST. LUCIE PRESS

A CRC Press Company
Boca Raton   London   New York   Washington, D.C.

Library of Congress Cataloging-in-Publication Data

Catalog record is available from the Library of Congress

Visit the CRC Press Web site at www.crcpress.com

© 1997 by CRC Press LLC
St. Lucie Press is an imprint of CRC Press LLC

No claim to original U.S. Government works
International Standard Book Number 1-57444-081-0
Printed in the United States of America   4 5 6 7 8 9 0
Printed on acid-free paper

This book is dedicated to my children,

Dawne and Joe

Their love and devotion has been the guiding force to my professional endeavors.

Their interest and involvement with helping and teaching others will be my legacy.

TABLE OF CONTENTS

FOREWORD

As a community college professor for the last fifteen years, I have taught medical law in the health sciences for seven of those years. I have reviewed many books in this discipline.

Professor Parelli's *Medicolegal Issues for Radiographers* is one of the better texts that I have read. It is focused on the field of radiologic technology. However, it can be useful to any person working in the area of imaging. The book is extremely relevant to the actual applications of law from the radiologic technologist's perspective. Professor Parelli has integrated tort law, labor law, legal doctrines, ethics, patient rights, risk management, and forensic radiology and has centered the vignettes around the radiographer and the radiology department.

Medicolegal Issues for Radiographers is clear, concise, and informative. Medical law is a course every healthcare professional should take, and to have a text centered on radiologic technology will be helpful to the student and the professional. The book is well written, and I would recommend it as a required text for any radiologic technology or imaging program.

Dana Brown-Klein, J.D., M.A.
Professor, Health Science
Cypress College

PREFACE

Since the first and second editions of this textbook were published, there has been a striking concern on the part of radiographers to understand and to resolve medicolegal and ethical problems that may be encountered daily.

Malpractice litigation has renewed and has increased the concerns for self-protection as well as patient care. The constant advances in technology have had an impact on the practice, attitudes, and moral values of all who participate in healthcare. The second and third editions have been developed to update the first edition of *Medicolegal Issues for Radiographers.*

Society, as well as the radiology science professional, is facing unprecedented ethical, legal, and moral dilemmas. Therefore, chapters on licensure, certification, and credentialing, as well as healthcare reform in mammography, were developed to address these controversial issues. Concepts on euthanasia and humanistic healthcare were added to the ethics section.

The vignettes presented in the first and second editions were exceptionally well received. Readers indicated that this was both an outstanding and unique feature of the textbook. Therefore, more vignettes have been developed to address radiographers' daily problems in their professional lives.

Certain specific areas of interest have been added to the second and third editions. These are: the Equal Employment Opportunity Act, sexual harassment, the Occupational Safety and Health Act, the Doctrine of Foreseeability, and risk management and liability.

It is hoped that the third edition will serve readers and colleagues in their endeavor to understand medicolegal issues and to be aware of and reduce any potential legal liability in the practice of radiology science.

Robert J. Parelli, M.A., R.T.(R)
Professor
Department of Radiologic Technology
Cypress College

AUTHOR

Robert J. Parelli, M.A., R.T.(R), has been the Program Director of the Department of Radiologic Technology at Cypress College since 1985 and has been an educator for 17 years. He has also served as the Radiology Department Manager at Los Alamitos Medical Center, Los Alamitos, California, and the Radiology Department Manager at Mercy General Hospital, Santa Ana, California. A former chairperson of the Education Committee, California Society of Radiologic Technologists, Mr. Parelli received his M.A. degree in Education from California State University, Long Beach, California and his R.T. certificate from St. Mary's Medical Center, Long Beach, California. Currently, he is an active member in the American Society of Radiologic Technologists, the California Society of Radiologic Technologists, and the Association of Educators in Radiology Sciences.

CHAPTER ONE

LEGAL DEFINITIONS

Upon completion of Chapter 1, the reader will be able to:

1. Define intentional torts.

2. Differentiate between assault and battery.

3. Recognize false imprisonment issues.

4. Discuss invasion of privacy situations.

5. Explain libel and slander.

6. Define unintentional misconduct and discuss the concepts of: (1) duty, (2) breach of care, (3) cause, and (4) injury.

7. Recognize malpractice situations.

Radiographers complete the work assigned each day without thinking about situations that could result in legal actions taken against them or against the health facility in which they work. As consumers become more aware concerning the standards of care they should be receiving, and are cognizant in seeking legal compensation when they do not receive an acceptable standard of care, radiographers must become knowledgeable of legal definitions of the standard of care.

The law that governs the relationships between individuals is known as *civil law*. The type of law that governs the rights between individuals in noncriminal actions is called *torts*. Torts are not easy to define, but a basic distinction is that they are violations of civil, as opposed to criminal, law. Tort law is personal injury law. The act may be malicious and intentional, or it may be the result of negligence and disregard for the rights of others. Torts include those conditions whereby the law allows for compensation to be paid an individual when that individual is damaged or injured by another. There are two types of torts—those resulting from intentional action and those resulting from unintentional action.

INTENTIONAL TORTS

There are several situations in which a tort action can be taken against the health professional because of some action that was deliberately taken. *Intentional tort* includes (1) civil assault, (2) civil battery, (3) false imprisonment, (4) libel and slander, and (5) invasion of privacy.

Assault

Assault is performing or threatening to perform intentional injury for bodily harm to another by administration of (1) poison, (2) anesthetics, (3) narcotics, or (4) willful and wrongful blows with weapons or other instruments. Assault is defined as the *threat* of touching in an injurious way. If the patient feels threatened and is caused to believe that he or she will be touched in a harmful manner, there may be justification for a charge of assault. To avoid this, it is absolutely essential that the radiographer explain what is going to happen and reassure the patient in any situation where the threat of harm may be an issue. Never use threats in an effort to gain the patient's cooperation. This statement applies when working with children as well as with adults. A tort of civil assault can be filed if a patient is apprehensive of injury by the imprudent conduct of the radiographer. If found guilty, the radiographer could be held liable or responsible to provide financial compensation to the patient for damages that may have resulted from any apprehension.

Battery

Battery consists of touching a person without permission. Again, a clear explanation of what is to be done is essential. If the patient refuses to be touched, that wish must be respected. Actually, battery implies that the touch is a wilful act to harm or provoke, but even the most well-intentioned touch may fall into this category if it has been expressly forbidden by the patient. This should not prevent the radiographer from placing a reassuring hand on the patient's shoulder, as long as the patient has not forbidden it, when there is no intent to harm or to invade the patient's privacy. On the other hand, a radiograph taken against the patient's will, or on the wrong patient, could be construed as battery. This emphasizes the need for consistently double checking patient identification. If a patient has refused a particular hypodermic injection and the nurse approaches the patient and attempts to administer the medication, it would be an assault. If the nurse administers the hypodermic injection, it would be a battery. The battery is the assault carried out or completed. Therefore, the patient must be conscious for an assault to occur. An unconscious patient may be the victim of a battery.

There are certain circumstances where an individual committing battery will not be liable for the battery. These are situations in which the conduct is said to be privileged, e.g., a radiographer restraining a patient who is obviously about to strike or injure other patients and/or himself/herself. The action of the radiographer to protect other patients and their interests outweighs the damage that may be sustained by restraining the patient and his/her interest.

VIGNETTE 1—ASSAULT AND BATTERY

A student and a staff radiographer were requested to perform an intravenous pyelogram on a 58-year-old woman with hypertension. The staff radiographer, who was the department clown, ordered the student technologist to load two 50cc syringes—one with contrast media, the other with isopropyl alcohol. The staff radiographer left the x-ray suite, leaving the student with the patient. The radiologist came into the room and grabbed one of the syringes without checking the empty contrast media vial. The radiologist injected the patient; upon completion of the injection, the patient immediately became comatose. The patient was sent to the intensive care unit. Blood chemistry, which was later ordered, indicated that the patient had a high concentration of alcohol in her blood. The radiologist was notified of the blood chemistry report by the patient's attending physician. The radiologist questioned both the staff radiographer and the student. The student told the radiologist that he was ordered to load two syringes, one with contrast media and the other with isopropyl alcohol.

Who would be held liable for assault and/or battery?

ANSWER

In any radiologic technology program, the student is under the guidance and direction of the radiology department personnel. The staff radiographer could be held liable for assault on the patient, and the radiologist could be held liable for battery. The radiologist failed to check the contents of the syringe by asking the student which one had contrast media or by checking the empty vial for the type of contrast and amount of concentration. The student would not be held liable because he was directed by the staff radiographer to load the two syringes with two different types of liquid. However, it is important to note that students should not be naive with regard to the types of contrast media used for certain radiographic procedures. The student should have told the radiologist the contents of both syringes prior to injection.

False Imprisonment

False imprisonment is intentional confinement without authorization by one who physically constricts a person using force, threat of force, or confining clothing or structures. False imprisonment becomes an issue when the patient wishes to leave and is not allowed to do so. Inappropriate use of physical restraints may also constitute false imprisonment. The confinement must be intentional and without legal justification. Freedom from unlawful restraint is a right protected by law. If the patient is improperly restrained, the law allows redress in the form of damages for this tort. The proof of all the elements of false imprisonment must be established in order to support that an illegal act was done. In situations where patients are a danger to themselves or to others, the patient may be restrained. A situation where false imprisonment may arise is when a radiographer uses a brat-board to restrain a child and does not tell the parents the reason for the restraint (Ward, 1985, p. 2).

Libel and Slander

Libel is written defamation of character. Oral defamation is termed slander. These are torts that affect the reputation and good name of another. The basic element of the tort of defamation is that the oral or written communication is made to another person other than the one defamed. The law does recognize certain relationships that require an individual be allowed to speak without fear of being sued for defamation of character, e.g., radiology department supervisors who must evaluate employees or give references regarding an employee's work have a qualified privilege.

Radiographers can protect themselves from this civil tort by using caution when conversing within the hearing distance of patients.

Invasion of Privacy

Invasion of privacy charges may result when confidentiality of information has not been maintained or when the patient's body has been improperly and unnecessarily exposed or touched. Protection of the patient's modesty is vitally important when performing radiographic procedures.

VIGNETTE 2—LIBEL, SLANDER, INVASION OF PRIVACY

A 16-year-old female was admitted through the emergency room with lower abdominal pain. The patient was transported to the x-ray department for an abdominal series. The orderly noticed on the x-ray request form under "pertinent clinical information" the abbreviation "PID." The orderly asked the staff radiographer what PID meant. The radiographer jokingly told the orderly that the patient had syphilis and ordered the orderly to wrap her up, as in an isolation procedure, for a communicable disease. The patient asked the orderly why she was being wrapped up with sheets and why the orderly was putting on gloves, a mask, and an isolation gown. The orderly told the patient that she had PID-syphilis, a communicable disease. On the way back to the x-ray department, the orderly sent a note to his friend in the central service department that a young female patient, who happened to be in the same high school class, had been admitted to the hospital with syphilis. Meanwhile, the young female patient became very distressed and told her father what the orderly had said to her. The father immediately contacted her attending physician to find out whether the daughter had syphilis. The doctor told the father that it was a mistake and that the orderly was wrong in telling the young girl that she had syphilis. Soon after the girl was treated and discharged from the hospital, the father filed a civil suit against the hospital for defamation of character.

Who, if anyone, was liable for slander? Libel? Why? Was the young female patient's privacy invaded?

ANSWER

The radiographer was liable for slander because he told the orderly (a second party) that the patient had syphilis, which was untrue. The patient became emotionally troubled when the orderly told her that she had syphilis. The orderly was held liable for libel since the written note that he sent to his friend in central services was defamatory. It is important to note that any information on the patient's chart, x-ray request form, or x-ray film is confidential information and not intended to be exposed to any other persons. Therefore, the young female patient's privacy had been invaded.

UNINTENTIONAL MISCONDUCT (NEGLIGENCE)

Whenever a radiographer unintentionally causes injury to a patient, it may be determined that a negligent act has been committed. Negligence refers to the neglect or omission of reasonable care or caution. The standard of reasonable care is based upon the "Doctrine of the Reasonably Prudent Man." This standard requires that a person perform as any reasonable man of ordinary prudence, with comparable education and skill, would perform under similar circumstances. In the relationship between a professional person and a patient or client, there is an implied contract to provide reasonable care. An act of negligence in the context of such a relationship is defined as *malpractice*. Negligence, as used in malpractice law, is not necessarily the same as *carelessness*. A person's conduct can be held negligent, in the legal sense, if a person acts carefully. For example, if a radiographer attempts a procedure for which he/she has had no prior training and does it carefully, the conduct, nevertheless, can be deemed negligent if harm results to the patient because the radiographer attempted the procedure without having had previous training and/or experience.

For a radiographer to be found negligent in a court and held liable for damages, the civil proceedings must establish the following elements:

1. *Duty* expected of the radiographer (standard of care).

2. *Breach* of duty by the radiographer.

3. *Cause* of injury due to the radiographer's negligence.

4. *Injury* to patient actually occurred.

The courts will interview experts in the field or workers in an occupation to determine if the proper standard of care has been followed.

Duty (Standard of Care)

If a physician instructs radiographer Parelli to radiograph Mrs. Ross's right leg, Parelli has a duty to properly radiograph patient Ross's right leg. When Parelli radiographs Ross's right leg, Parelli will have performed as a reasonable and prudent radiographer would have acted under similar circumstances. However, if Parelli radiographs Ross's *left* leg, Parelli is breaching the standard of care by failing to follow the physician's directions.

Breach of Care

What if Parelli's radiographs of Ross's right leg were not adequate to provide a diagnosis? The radiographer has a duty to ensure that radiographs are clear and of the highest quality for the physician's diagnosis. Then, Parelli's inadequate radiographs are a breach of the radiographer's duty. If Ross's condition deteriorates because the physician could not properly interpret the radiograph, then Ross would have grounds to sue the physician and Parelli. This would be resolved in court with the assistance of expert witnesses and by the judgment of a jury on a case-by-case basis.

Cause

The radiographer's negligence may be the direct cause of the patient's injury. The radiographer has the duty to make sure that a dizzy or semiconscious patient does not fall from the x-ray table. It would be a breach of duty if the radiographer left the x-ray room. Leaving the room would be closely related to the patient's falling from the table.

Injury

A patient sustains actual injury. If a patient falls from the x-ray table because the radiographer leaves the room, but the patient is not injured, the patient cannot expect to receive compensation for nonexistent injuries. A personal injury or tort will not be successful in establishing liability if there are no damages.

To determine if negligence exists, the court will determine if a "reasonable man" could have anticipated the harmful results. A reasonable man is defined as a man of average prudence, using ordinary care and skill, who provides a standard of care or a standard of behavior. The court will interview experts in the field or workers in an occupation to determine if the proper standard of care has been followed.

A duty to protect another is proportional to the risk or hazard of a particular activity. A person is negligent when, without intending any harm or wrong, he/she does such an act or omits to take the necessary precautions that, under ordinary circumstances, he/she ought to reasonably foresee, and this act will thereby expose the interest of another to unreasonable risk or harm. A standard of care requires each person to conduct himself/herself as an average, "reasonable" person would do in similar circumstances.

Proximate or legal cause must show a connection between the act and the resultant injury or harm. A cause-effect relationship must exist, and the cause must be substantial enough to lead reasonable men to conclude it is indeed the cause of harm. A plaintiff cannot recover unless actual injury is suffered and he/she is able to show actual loss or damages resulting from the defendant's act.

The common defenses against negligence are:

1. Contributory negligence.

2. Comparative negligence.

3. Assumption of risk.

Contributory negligence is a situation where the patient failed to act as a reasonable and prudent person would, and this negligence contributed to the injury. Comparative negligence occurs when the plaintiff fault is equal to that of the defendant's, although some states allow for degrees of negligence and allow recovery based on the relative degree of fault.

Assumption of risk is when the patient or plaintiff, by expressed or implied consent or agreement, recognizes the danger and assumes the risk. These legal defenses against negligence demonstrate the importance of providing detailed incident reports with an accurate documentation of the sequence of events, gaining the patient's or guardian's signature on a consent form, informing the patient of the procedure, and giving accurate instructions while performing the radiographic procedure.

MALPRACTICE

Malpractice lawsuits against physicians and hospitals are becoming increasingly common. Legally, to establish a claim of malpractice, a claimant must prove to the satisfaction of the court that three things are true:

1. The patient has sustained some loss, damage, or injury.

2. The person or institution being sued is the party at fault or responsible for the loss.

3. The loss is attributable to negligence or improper practice.

Accordingly, a patient may sustain some loss, but to collect damages, the court must be convinced that the loss is due to negligence in professional care or treatment. Usually a determination of negligence is based on whether or not the usual standards and procedures for that particular situation were followed in the case in question. In another case, a patient may prove that someone was negligent but may not be entitled to a settlement unless it can be demonstrated that a loss has occurred as a result. Nonetheless, it is inexcusable to be complacent about negligence simply because there was "no harm done." Nor should one be callous about a loss as long as accepted and established procedures were followed.

There has been much discussion concerning whether radiographers should carry malpractice insurance. Hospitals nearly always carry liability insurance that covers employees. It is essential that radiographers learn the extent of provisions for malpractice coverage in their institutions. According to the legal "Doctrine of Respondeat Superior (let the master respond)," the employer is liable for the negligent acts of employees that occur in the course of their work. When a physician is supervising and controlling the activities of a hospital employee, his/her authority and responsibility will supersede that of the employer according to the "Doctrine of Borrowed Servant." Regardless of how these legal doctrines may be applied, the fundamental rule of law that every radiographer should clearly know and understand is that *each person is liable for his/her own negligent conduct.* This is called the "Doctrine of Personal Liability." It means that the law does not allow the wrongdoer to escape responsibility even though someone else may be sued and held legally responsible. In some cases, hospital insurers who had paid malpractice claims have successfully recovered damages from negligent employees by filing separate lawsuits against them. This would be sufficient reason for radiographers to be protected by their own liability insurance policies. Other radiographers argue that the potential for a large insurance settlement is an incentive to sue and that if the radiographer has no means of paying a large claim, there will be no suit. The American Society of Radiologic Technologists offers professional liability coverage on a group basis. The possibility of losing personal assets, such as one's home, may provide motivation for joining such a plan.

SAMPLE CASE: STATE LIABLE FOR FALSE IMPRISONMENT OF PATIENT

The state was liable for false imprisonment, negligence, and malpractice arising out of a patient's involuntary commitment to a state hospital, a New York appellate court ruled.

The patient was admitted to a general hospital for treatment of a gallbladder problem. Her history included emotional problems based on marital difficulties with suicide attempts.

After a series of tests, including consultation with a psychiatrist, the patient was informed that her gallbladder would be removed. Later that same day, her physician told her to dress and pack because he had arranged for her to be admitted to the state hospital. State troopers handcuffed her, strapped her in the seat of a troop car, and took her to the state hospital accompanied by a female hospital employee.

On arrival at the state hospital, the admitting officer realized that the physician lacked the requisite authority to order the patient's involuntary commitment. He asked her to sign a voluntary admission form, but she refused, protesting her presence there.

The admitting officer ignored the patient's complaints and assigned her to a ward without a proper physical or psychiatric examination and without contacting her family or her physician. She remained in the hospital over the weekend.

In a suit against the state, the patient was awarded $40,000, and her husband's derivation claim was dismissed. On appeal, the court said that for an acutely medically ill person, the episode justified money damages for false imprisonment, along with an additional sum for the residual effects attributable solely to the negligence of state agents. Affirming the lower court's judgment, the court found that her husband did not sustain his burden of proof (*Plumadore* v. *State of New York,* 427 NYS 2d 90 NY Supreme Court, Appellate Division, April 24, 1980).

REVIEW QUESTIONS

1. A deliberate attempt, or threat, with force or violence directed toward the person of another to corporal injury is:

   a.   Battery.

   b.   Malice.

   c.   Assault.

   d.   Tort.

2. An injury or civil wrong committed with or without force to the person or property of another is:

   a.   Battery.

   b.   Malice.

   c.   Assault.

   d.   Tort.

3. Written defamation of character is:

   a.   Libel.

   b.   Slander.

   c.   Invasion of privacy.

   d.   False imprisonment.

4. Touching a person without permission is:

   a.   Battery.

   b.   Malice.

   c.   Assault.

   d.   Tort.

5. Inappropriate use of physical restraints may constitute:

    a.   Slander.

    b.   Malice.

    c.   Invasion of privacy.

    d.   False imprisonment.

6. Negligence or omission of reasonable care is:

    a.   Carelessness.

    b.   Negligence.

    c.   Libel.

    d.   Tort.

7. For a radiographer to be found negligent in court, the civil proceedings must establish the following elements *except*:

    a.   Carelessness.

    b.   Duty.

    c.   Cause.

    d.   Injury.

8. A radiographer's failure to produce quality radiographs for physician interpretation would be considered failure of which one of the four elements that contribute to negligent acts?

    a.   Duty.

    b.   Breach.

    c.   Cause.

    d.   Injury.

9. Which of the four elements that contribute to negligent acts would apply if the radiographer left the x-ray room and the patient falls off of the x-ray table?

    a.   Duty.

    b.   Breach.

    c.   Cause.

    d.   Injury.

10. Oral defamation of one's character is:

    a.   Libel.

    b.   Slander.

    c.   Invasion of privacy.

    d.   False imprisonment.

CHAPTER TWO

LEGAL DOCTRINES

Upon completion of Chapter 2, the reader will be able to:

1. Explain the Doctrine of Personal Liability.

2. Examine the Doctrine of Respondeat Superior.

3. Interpret the Doctrine of Borrowed Servant.

4. Apply the Doctrine of Res Ipsa Loquitur to the legal case of *Ybarra* v. *Spangard*.

5. Assess the Doctrine of Foreseeability to equipment safety.

6. Apply the provisions of the Safe Medical Devices Act to the Doctrine of Foreseeability.

Should radiographers be concerned about the risk they may or may not have in being named as a defendant in a medical malpractice suit? Things do go wrong and mistakes are made. In radiology, it might have been that a patient fell from a radiographic table or tripped getting into a wheelchair. It might have been a reaction to contrast media or an embolism as a result of a special procedure. It might have been a perforated rectum after a barium enema. It might have been a misdiagnosed radiograph that resulted in a delay in treatment or even surgery on the wrong side. It might have been an examination done on the wrong patient. It might have been and has been a thousand other things.

The legal responsibility of the radiographer is to be a radiographer of safe care. The various legal doctrines will give insight into the ways in which the law fixes liability for acts of malpractice and will show how a radiographer may be subjected to a greater degree of liability based upon various factors, or doctrines of law, or legal status of a radiographer's employer.

DOCTRINE OF PERSONAL LIABILITY

If there is one rule that every radiographer should know and clearly understand, it is the fundamental rule of law that every person is liable for his/her own negligent conduct. This is known as the "Doctrine of Personal Liability." This means that the law does not permit a wrongdoer to avoid legal liability for his/her own wrongdoing even though someone else may also be sued and held legally liable for the wrongful conduct in question under another rule of law; it will not negate one's own responsibility.

Although the radiographer cannot be held liable for the actions of the hospital or that of a physician or radiologist, the radiographer can be held responsible and liable for his/her own negligent actions if named in a suit.

VIGNETTE 3—PERSONAL LIABILITY

Suppose a supervising radiographer directs a staff radiographer to perform a radiographic procedure, such as a mammogram, which the staff radiographer is not qualified to perform. Assume the staff radiographer follows the order without question and harm occurs to the patient; assume that the supervising radiographer knows, or should have known, the radiographer is not qualified.

In this event, if the supervising radiographer is found liable, would the staff radiographer be relieved of liability?

ANSWER

The answer is no, and the converse is true. The staff radiographer should know his/her own qualifications and limitations. The staff radiographer would be personally liable for performing a radiographic examination that injured a patient and for which the staff radiographer is not qualified. The supervising radiographer would be liable for assigning the function to the staff radiographer when the supervising radiographer knows that the staff radiographer is not normally qualified to perform mammographic procedures. However, assume the supervising radiographer directs the staff radiographer to perform a routine radiograph which he/she is ordinarily able to perform. For example, the staff radiographer is assigned to perform a chest x-ray. While performing the chest x-ray, the staff radiographer pushes the patient's chin up to the wall bucky device and bruises the patient's chin. Since the patient received injury, the staff radiographer has been negligent in positioning the patient for the chest exam and injuring the patient's chin. Where does the liability rest in this case? In this set of facts, only the staff radiographer would be held liable for negligence in carrying out an assignment clearly within the staff radiographer's capabilities. The supervising radiographer has the right to expect the staff radiographers to be capable of performing radiographic procedures without injury to the patient. The supervising radiographer has the right to assume that his/her co-workers are competent unless put on notice to the contrary.

DOCTRINE OF RESPONDEAT SUPERIOR

The "Doctrine of Respondent Superior (let the master answer)" is a legal doctrine which holds an employer liable for the negligent acts of employees that occur while they are carrying out his/her orders or otherwise serving his/her interests. As early as 1698, courts declared that a master must respond to injuries and losses of third persons caused by the master's servants. The nineteenth century courts adopted the phrase *respondeat superior,* "let the master respond," which is "obviously founded on the great principle of social duty, that every man, in the management of his own affairs, whether by himself or by his agents or servants, shall so conduct them as not to injure another" (*Farwell* v. *Boston W.R. Corporation,* 45 Mass 49, 1842).

SAMPLE CASE: *SIMPSON V. SISTERS OF CHARITY OF PROVIDENCE IN OREGON*

This is the most involved case of the Doctrine of Respondeat Superior and radiographers. Mr. Simpson, the plaintiff, fell off of a six-foot scaffold, landing on his back, neck, and shoulders. On admission to the hospital's emergency room, the physician on duty ordered radiographs of both wrists, both forearms, AP chest, thoracic spine, cervical spine, and skull. Several radiographers began taking films at 12:30 P.M. They had difficulty obtaining films of the cervicothoracic area, and ultimately six or seven "swimmer's views" were done. The plaintiff also had a pre-existing rheumatoid spondylitis condition that made it difficult to radiograph this area. As a result, "no clear x-rays of the cervicothoracic junction were obtained."

Nevertheless, there was testimony in court that without moving the plaintiff and by making minor adjustments to the x-ray equipment, the radiographers could have obtained a good view of the junction. In fact, films of the area taken at a later date were of diagnostic quality. Radiographs were stopped at 2:20 P.M. on the night of admission because the plaintiff's physician believed that the x-rays taken were the best that could be obtained under the circumstances.

The plaintiff was immobilized from the time he arrived at the hospital. But there is evidence that this immobilization caused lung congestion. For this reason, the neurologist ordered the patient "dangled" (i.e., patient sat on the bed with legs over the side). It was later determined that the plaintiff had a fracture at the cervicothoracic junction, and this movement compressed the spinal cord, paralyzing the plaintiff from the shoulders down.

The plaintiff brought suit against the physician and the hospital. He settled out of court with the physician for $150,000, leaving only the hospital as defendant. The hospital's liability, if any, would be based on vicarious liability through the Doctrine of Respondeat Superior, i.e., the hospital as employer would be held liable. The hospital on appeal had three major legal arguments because of its employees' negligence, if any:

1. The hospital's radiographers were not negligent because they were following orders.

2. The radiographers were under the supervision and control of the treating physicians.

3. There was no causation in fact between the failure to demonstrate the fracture and the ambulation of the patient.

Regarding the second issue, in the evidence by a preponderance, it was found that the radiographers were not under doctor's orders as to the radiographic technique employed in taking and developing films. "There was no radiologist in the x-ray room while the radiographers were performing their duties and normally the radiologist does not see or consult with the patients" (Warner, 1981, p. 28).

The attending physician testified that he did not give the radiographers instructions concerning the milliamperage to be used or the use of grids. In fact, he testified, "...I would never attempt to offer advice to the technologist" (Warner, 1981, p. 28). Testimony also confirmed that the radiographers must follow a departmental routine, which is based on, and even cites portions of, "Merrill, Vol. 1, pp. 218–237 and Merrill, Vol. 1, pp. 238–245" (Warner, 1981, p. 28). The court then dealt with the issue of the radiographers' alleged negligence. The court reasoned:

> The jury could believe the evidence that showed the x-ray technicians to be negligent in failing to obtain a clear film of the cervical thoracic junction and that the technicians were not following the physician's orders as to technique...the jury could have found from the evidence that the orders (request for films) were not carried out in a competent manner. An expert witness testified that diagnostic films could have been originally taken and this was supported by the evidence that, in fact, diagnostic films were taken at a later date... *The jury could have found from the evidence that for x-ray technicians to meet the standard of care expected of them, it is not enough for them to take a series of bad pictures hoping to obtain a good one* (Warner, 1981, p. 28).

The Supreme Court of Oregon affirmed the lower court's decision, and the plaintiff won. The hospital was held liable because its employees, the radiographers, were negligent within the scope of their duties. The radiographers were not named as defendants in this case, but it is clear that they could have been.

This case is of particular interest to radiographers because the radiographers' actions were held to be negligent because they failed to meet the standard of care requirements for their particular occupation. It was shown in court that, in fact, the radiographers should have been able to secure a diagnostic radiograph. The technologist's inability to get such a film, even after many attempts, was a failure to meet the standard of care.

It should be noted that in this case a radiologist was not present, nor did a radiologist make the decision that stopped further attempts to obtain a diagnostic view of the cervicothoracic junction. The court in a footnote even notes that, under more typical circumstances, such a decision should lie with the radiologist (*Simpson* v. *Sisters of Charity of Providence in Oregon*, 588 P 2nd 4, Oregon Superior Court, December 19, 1978).

The Doctrine of Respondeat Superior applies only when there is an employee/employer relationship and only with respect to negligent acts committed within the scope of that employment. The theory behind the doctrine is that one who is an employer should be held legally responsible for the conduct of those employees whose actions he is obligated to direct or control. Often the critical test in determining liability is who had control over the employee. For example, Barbara Barium, R.T., is performing a shoulder radiograph. Barbara Barium proceeds to grab the patient's arm and forcefully externally rotates the patient's shoulder, causing it to become dislocated. Who is liable?

Both Barbara Barium and the employer, Roentgen Memorial Medical Center, may be held liable if Barbara is a bona fide employee and was performing the radiographic examination assigned by the medical center as a proper function for which she is qualified. Roentgen Memorial Medical Center or her employer is liable for all negligent acts committed that are related to the function of the radiographer in the service of the employer.

SAMPLE CASE: SURGEON AND HOSPITAL LIABLE FOR BURN FROM X-RAY UNIT

An award of $25,000 that was made to an elderly patient who was burned by an x-ray machine during surgery was found not to be excessive by a Louisiana appellate court. The court found that the burn was the result of negligence by both the hospital employee (radiographer) and a surgeon.

In August 1973, the patient, 68, was operated on for a hip injury. While she was anesthetized during the operation, the surgeon manipulated her leg so that it came in contact with an x-ray machine, resulting in a second or third degree burn on the anterior medial aspect of her left thigh. The machine was under the sole control of two student radiographers, who either because of an assistant surgeon's instructions or because of a misunderstanding taped the collimator light switch in an "on" position, thus preventing a safety mechanism from working and allowing the machine to overheat.

The patient, a registered nurse, brought an action against the hospital and the surgeon, who died before trial. The patient testified that the burn was still bothering her. She showed the scar on her thigh to the jury, testifying that it caused her embarrassment when swimming and wearing shorts in the summer. The jury found both the surgeon and the hospital employees negligent.

On appeal, the appellate court said the patient's injury was not an ordinary risk of major surgery and that it could have been prevented by the exercise of proper care. Both the hospital and the doctor were under a duty to guard the unconscious patient against being burned by contact with the overheated x-ray machine, the court said. The hospital was negligent in failing to properly supervise its student radiographers. These technicians were negligent in allowing the collimator to overheat, and the surgeon was negligent in manipulating the patient's leg into contact with the x-ray machine, the court said.

As to the contention that the amount of damages was excessive because the patient had no loss of wages and did not have a long life expectancy, the court said that the patient was entitled to be free of unnecessary pain during her last years, and the mere fact of being 72 makes each year of life more precious to her.

Affirming the trial court's decision, the court also pointed out that pride in appearance was not the sole prerogative of the young (*Barber* v. *St. Francis Cabrini Hospital, Inc.,* 345 P 2nd 1307, Los Angeles Court of Appeals, May 13, 1977, in *The Citation,* 38(5), October 1977).

DOCTRINE OF BORROWED SERVANT

The borrowed servant doctrine is usually considered when discussing the respondeat superior principle. In the borrowed servant doctrine, as the name implies, the employee is "borrowed" for a particular purpose or agency. The classical example occurs in the operating room. Although the scrub nurse or operating room technician is an employee of the hospital, he/she is paid and controlled by the administration of the hospital for the purpose of a specific operation. But that same employee is directed or controlled by the surgeon during the operation; therefore, depending on the facts of the case, the negligent liability of the scrub technician may vicariously involve the surgeon performing the operation rather than the hospital that employs the technician. Here the law infers that the one directing or controlling the actions of the employee has the greater responsibility over the one who merely pays the employee. For example, the scrub technician is asked for a surgical count of sponges at the end of an operative procedure. Assume that the surgeon has control and directs the count of the sponges and makes the final decision regarding the accuracy of the count. If the count is wrong and a sponge is left in the patient, both the scrub technician and the doctor would be liable. This is referred to as the "captain of the ship doctrine." The captain of the ship has traditionally been held responsible for all those under his supervision. Similarly, the surgeon who controls the actions of the assisting doctors, anesthetist, and the technician is considered the "captain of the ship" in the operating room. The Doctrine of Borrowed Servant can be applied to the radiographer who is performing radiographic procedures under the guidance and direction of the radiologist. The radiologist must be involved in the daily performance of radiographers and see to it that they perform their duties properly. Radiologists, although present in the department, are frequently not around for particular radiological studies. This is particularly true when plain films are obtained, but also applies to several other studies including fluoroscopy, excretory urography, ultrasound, CT scanning, and MRI. Technologists are given various degrees of responsibility, depending upon the skill of the technologist and the particular radiologist and institution. The physician cannot, however, delegate his/her own duties to the technologist. In fact, it is foreseeable that in circumstances where a physician is directly in charge of a case or particular area, this may be viewed somewhat like an operating room where the physician may have a greater duty to supervise the technologist working with him/her. Such areas might be the angiography and special procedures suites, as well as the CT, ultrasound, and MRI sections. The courts may find it easier to envision that a hospital-employed radiographer comes under the control of the radiologists in the department. In a negligence suit against the radiographer, the hospital may attempt to go after the radiology group or radiologist in charge for indemnification or compensation for any loss.

VIGNETTE 4—LEAVING A PATIENT UNATTENDED

A patient with nausea was left unattended on an x-ray table after radiographs were taken. Upon entering the room, the radiographer heard groans and thought the patient was vomiting in the bathroom. Instead, they found the patient lying on the floor beside the x-ray table. The patient filed a civil suit against the hospital.

What legal doctrines, if any, would apply in this case? Who would be vicariously liable (Hospital Authority of Hall County v. Adams, 140 SE 2nd 139, Georgia, 1964)?

ANSWER

The court stated that the radiographer should have foreseen that the patient, because of his nausea, might attempt to go to the bathroom and injure himself in the process, especially since he was on medication that might affect his movements and coordination. The Doctrine of Respondeat Superior implies that it is the hospital's duty to exercise reasonable care while attending to patients as the particular condition requires. The radiographer could be held vicariously liable under the Doctrine of Personal Liability; the radiographer can be held liable for his own negligence. Patients, on no occasion, should be left alone in the x-ray suite.

DOCTRINE OF RES IPSA LOQUITUR

There are certain cases of negligence in which the defendant is required to prove innocence. Res ipsa loquitur means "the thing speaks for itself." In this process, a case is built around evidence demonstrating that an injury could not have occurred if there had been no negligence. In a surgical procedure, for example, it is discovered that a pair of forceps has been left in the patient's abdomen. That the forceps are in the patient is a provable fact. They were not in the patient before surgery, and they could be in the patient only as a result of negligence on the part of the surgical team. As another example, a patient's being exposed to radiation sufficient to cause skin lesions could result only from negligence on the part of the radiographer. In these cases, the procedures begin with the facts of evidence and proceed to establish that these facts would not have been true if there had not been negligence on someone's part. In these circumstances, it is incumbent upon the defendants to demonstrate that they were not the party responsible for the negligent act.

SAMPLE CASE: *YBARRA V. SPANGARD*

The oldest of the res ipsa loquitur cases goes back to 1944. Plaintiff Joseph Ybarra brought an action for damages for personal injuries allegedly inflicted on the plaintiff by Dr. Lawrence C. Spangard and other physicians and nurses. Mr. Ybarra, upon referral by Dr. Tilley, entered a hospital owned and managed by defendant Dr. Swift. Dr. Spangard was to perform an appendectomy. Mr. Ybarra was given a hypodermic injection, slept, and later was awakened by Drs. Tilley and Spangard and was wheeled into the operating room by nurse (defendant) Gisler, an employee of Dr. Swift. Defendant Dr. Reser, the anesthetist, also an employee of Dr. Swift, adjusted plaintiff for the operation by pulling his body to the head of the operating table and, according to plaintiff's testimony, laying him back against two hard objects at the tip of his shoulders. Dr. Reser administered the anesthetic and the plaintiff lost consciousness. When he awoke early the following morning, he was in his hospital room attended by defendant nurse Thompson, the special nurse, and another nurse not made a defendant.

When plaintiff awakened, he felt a sharp pain about halfway between his neck and the point of his right shoulder. He was given diathermy treatments for the pain, but it spread down his arm, and he developed paralysis and atrophy of the muscles about the shoulder.

Plaintiff sued all physicians and nurses involved in his case (but for one), and he sued the physician-owner of the hospital. At trial court in California, judgment was made in favor of the defendant, and the plaintiff appealed the decision. The appeal was made before the Supreme Court of California. The Supreme Court reversed the decision, finding for the plaintiff. A finding for the plaintiff means that the court found all defendants jointly and severally liable for the damages done. But it is obvious from the facts that all defendants were not equally culpable. Surely not all defendants caused the injury. It could have been one person, two, or more. But certainly the gunshot approach used in naming defendants included some "innocent" parties with whoever was "guilty." In fact, in testimony, "each testified that while he was present he saw nothing occur." How could the court reach such a seemingly unfair result?

The legal theory upon which *Ybarra* was presented was negligence including the doctrine of res ipsa loquitur. Application of the doctrine of res ipsa is relatively recent. The classic example is a sponge or forceps left in an abdomen following surgery. The result is such that it would not have occurred but for some negligence. No expert testimony is necessary; laymen know that with properly conducted medical practices, such results do not occur (Warner, 1981, p. 28).

To apply the doctrine of res ipsa loquitur, certain conditions must be met:

1. The accident would not have occurred if reasonable care had been used.

2. The instrumentality must be under the exclusive control of the defendant(s).

3. The plaintiff did not contribute in some way to the accident.

The decision in *Ybarra* was precedent setting on its facts, since no one ever found out "who did the dastardly deed." It is now virtually the standard analysis today. This decision and others like it encourage plaintiffs to use the shotgun approach in naming defendants.

There are a number of reasons why a plaintiff's attorney may want to name a radiographer in a res ipsa loquitur case:

1. To meet the elements of res ipsa as discussed in the Ybarra case.

2. When the "big pocket" hospital or physicians are unavailable, because various immunities are applied to the hospital

or because the radiographer was not, in fact, controlled by the physician.

3. When the hospital and/or physician cannot be sued as defendant because they were not directly negligent, nor can vicarious liability be applied.

4. When it is desirable due to trial tactics such as the plaintiff being able to require deposition of defendants, while deposition of mere witnesses is voluntary.

5. To place pressure on the radiographer to encourage his/her pretrial testimony and in-court testimony as a witness.

6. When it is presumed by the plaintiff that, in fact, the radiographer has assets or insurance.

7. When it aids or is essential to the case.

SAMPLE CASE: RES IPSA LOQUITUR INSTRUCTION PROPER IN SUIT AGAINST SURGEON WHO CUT BLADDER

A trial court should have instructed a jury on the res ipsa loquitur doctrine in a malpractice action by a patient whose bladder was inadvertently cut during an exploratory laparotomy, the New Jersey Supreme Court ruled.

The 36-year-old patient, a registered nurse, had a history of gynecological and urinary problems. She had a urethrocele and rectocele surgically corrected in 1973, and following complaints of profuse vaginal bleeding, she underwent a total abdominal hysterectomy on March 31, 1975. A few days later, she developed pain in the right side of her abdomen, radiating into the groin and thigh. An exploratory laparotomy was recommended because an unexplained mass was discovered in the right lower quadrant of her abdomen.

During the laparotomy, the surgeon cut into her bladder by mistake. The bladder was not in its normal position, and it was under a substantial amount of scar tissue from previous operations. Bleeding and a urinary fistula developed, and at the time of trial in July 1978, she suffered recurrent infections, burning, chronic cystitis, and muscle spasms. In a malpractice action against the operating surgeon, a trial court concluded that she failed to establish by expert testimony that the physician was negligent. The decision was affirmed on appeal.

Reversing the lower court, the Supreme Court said that expert medical testimony established sufficient direct proof of the surgeon's negligence to support a jury verdict on liability. There was expert testimony that it was common knowledge within the medical community that cutting the bladder did not ordinarily occur in the absence of the surgeon's negligence. This testimony was sufficient to support a jury instruction on res ipsa loquitur, which the trial court did not give, the court said (*Bucklew* v. *Grossbard,* 425 A.2d 1150 New Jersey Supreme Court, October 14, 1981, in *The Citation,* 44(9), February 15, 1982).

SAMPLE CASE: HOSPITAL PATIENT AWARDED $1,290 FOR X-RAY INJURY

A jury award of $1,290 to a patient on whom a fluoroscopic spot film device fell was not erroneous, a Texas appellate court ruled.

The patient was undergoing x-ray examination on April 18, 1974, when the cable supporting the device broke and fell on him. He sued the hospital, the radiologist, and others. The patient claimed that the device caused injury to his back. A jury awarded him $786 for loss of past earnings and $504 for past physical pain and suffering. The jury found no loss of future earning capacity and no compensable loss for future pain and suffering. The patient appealed on the grounds of inadequacy of the verdict.

Affirming the decision, the appellate court said that the evidence supported the findings of the trial court. There was testimony that the patient complained of leg pain, not back pain, after the accident. A physician testified that the patient had complained of a back injury before the accident. The patient did not see a physician for 18 days after the injury, and it was more than a month before he first complained of back pain to his physician. A neurosurgeon described his symptoms as nonphysiological, and his physician noted that a back brace he prescribed looked unused six months later. Further, in the two years after the accident, the patient made considerably more money than in the year of the accident and the previous year, the court said (*Partida* v. *Park North General Hospital,* 592 SW 2d 38 Texas Court of Civil Appeals, November 15, 1978, in *The Citation,* 40(5), December 15, 1979).

VIGNETTE 5—NEGLIGENCE FOUND IN X-RAY PATIENT'S FALL FROM TABLE

A university was obligated to indemnify a medical clinic for the negligence of a university employee working at the clinic, a Hawaii appellate court ruled.

A patient was admitted to the clinic for a barium enema. A university student, acting under the general supervision of the clinic's employees, attached the standard footrest to an x-ray table and placed the patient on the table. When a physician employed by the clinic tilted the table, the footrest detached, and the patient fell. He was severely injured. The clinic agreed to settle the patient's claim against it for $150,690.80.

The clinic then sued the university for indemnity under the agreement between them. Under the agreement, students in a radiology technology program at the university obtained clinical experience at the clinic. The university agreed to indemnify the clinic from claims and expenses for negligent acts of its employees and students. A jury found the clinic 70 percent responsible and the university 30 percent responsible for the patient's injuries.

On appeal, the decision was affirmed. The university was ordered to pay the clinic 30 percent of the settlement amount and of the clinic's $57,913.01 costs and fees. The court said that indemnity was not limited to damages caused solely by a student or employee of the university (*Straub Clinic and Hospital, Inc.* v. *Chicago Insurance Company,* 665 P2d 176 Hawaii Intermediate Court of Appeals, June 8, 1983).

What legal doctrine(s) would apply in this case? Could the clinic and/ or university file a suit against the employee and/or student to recover damages?

ANSWER

The legal doctrine that applies in this case is *Respondent Superior*, the clinic is responsible for the negligent acts of the university employee and student. Through the agreement between the clinic and the university, the university paid all damages from the negligent acts of the employee and student. Both the clinic and university could file suit against the employee and student to indemnify the university from claims and expenses for negligent acts of its employees. Students are under the direct supervision of the university employee and/or clinic employee. The student would not be liable for any indemnity claims.

The specter of medical malpractice suits for radiographers is, at present, small, timid, and barely reaching its infancy. The possibility of a medical malpractice or negligence suit against a radiographer does exist. It is advisable that the practice of "defensive" radiography is a must. Defensive technology should include:

1. *Adherence to reasonably prudent practice.* The radiographer must be aware that as a trained individual with specialized knowledge and skills he/she is expected, both ethically and legally, to practice those skills and apply the knowledge of a reasonably prudent and reasonably competent practitioner of radiography. The radiographer should become a cautious, conservative practitioner conscientiously aware of what he/she is doing and the possible consequences of his/her actions.

2. *Safeguarding, to every extent possible, the legal rights and welfare of the patient.* By actively protecting the legal rights and welfare of the patient, the radiographer is literally protecting himself/herself. By protecting the patient's right to consent, right to be safe, etc., radiographers fulfill their own duties to the patient.

3. *Acquiring malpractice or negligence insurance coverage.* Substitute the insurance company's big pocket for the radiographer's little pocket. For example, if the patient-plaintiff is desperate, a little pocket does look better than nothing. Not only

is the plaintiff pitted against the defendants, but often defendant is pitted against defendant. Each employee in the hospital will have $1,500,000 of malpractice liability insurance coverage with the hospital as long as the radiographer is employed at the hospital/clinic. The hospital may try to insulate itself from vicarious liability by arguing that the radiographer acted "outside the scope of his/her duties." The physician may try to insulate himself from vicarious liability by arguing that the radiographer was not in the supervision and control of the physician at the time of the accident. Or the radiographer may want to argue that the accident was caused by the corporate negligence of the hospital due to inadequate staffing, lack of facilities or supplies, or lack of consultation or supervision (Warner, 1981, p. 29).

It would be advisable for radiographers to check with the hospital administration/physician office/clinic to determine if they are named either as individuals or as a class in the hospital malpractice insurance policy. On investigating this point, the radiographer would do well to see the policy itself and those portions showing the groups covered, the extent of coverage (policy limits), and activities covered (Bundy, 1988, p. 192).

DOCTRINE OF FORESEEABILITY

This is a principle of law that holds an individual liable for all the natural and proximate consequences of any negligent acts to another individual to whom a duty is owed and which could, or should, have been reasonably foreseen under the circumstances. A simple definition is that an individual could reasonably foresee that certain action or inaction on his/her part could result in injury to another individual. It also means that the injury actually suffered must be related to the foreseeable injury. Routine equipment check is important in overcoming this doctrine.

Routine Equipment Check

It is a basic understanding of hospital care that equipment used for, and by, patients should be safe and function properly. The hospital must have some type of system, such as a quality control program, to routinely check equipment and supplies so that all are maintained in proper working order. It is evident that any reasonably prudent professional radiographer could foresee that harm could come to a patient if equipment is not checked and tested properly.

"The Snitch Law"

Under a new law, stiff fines could be imposed on radiographers who do not report deaths and serious injuries or illnesses caused by defects in medical products. The *Safe Medical Devices Act* of 1991, for the first time, will authorize civil penalties to radiographers who do not report defects and failures in medical devices. Violations could result in fines of $15,000 per violation to a maximum of $1 million per case. The act will force hospitals to report problems they have been reluctant to report due to lack of time or liability questions.

More specifically, the act imposes new record keeping and reporting requirements on manufacturers, distributors, and healthcare workers. Key provisions of the law include:

1. Every healthcare provider is obligated to report defects and failures of medical products directly to the Food and Drug Administration (FDA).

2. All manufacturers will be obligated to report any complaints they receive as well as any defects they themselves find in products to the FDA.

3. A six-month summary report of problems must be sent by the medical facility to the FDA. This is a check and balance system. It ensures that the FDA is receiving all reports from the manufacturers.

4. Failure of healthcare workers to report problems could result in substantive fines.

The FDA has indicated that the radiographer will now be more susceptible to direct liability.

VIGNETTE 6—DEFECTIVE X-RAY EQUIPMENT

Richard Rem, R.T., has been working at Roentgen Memorial Medical Center for over five years. During this time, Richard Rem was told that one of the qualities of a professional radiographer is the ability to improvise. Richard Rem has been "improvising" as necessity indicates all of his professional life. There were often times when equipment was not adequate, and Richard Rem always managed with the equipment provided to him by a hospital administration.

He has been assigned to perform portable chest x-rays on patients in the intensive care unit. The source to image distance indicator ruler, which is placed on the x-ray tube collimator, has broken off. Richard Rem is unable to accurately adjust the source to image receptor distance to the approximate 72 inches. Richard has extended both of his arms between the patient and the x-ray tube, which is positioned at the foot of the patient's bed. Richard's arms extended measures 68 inches. On the next shift change, Richard Rem tells Sally Sievert, R.T., that the source to image distance indicator ruler has broken off the x-ray tube collimator. Richard tells Sally that the portable x-ray machine could be used if Sally extends her arms out between the patient and the x-ray tube to provide 72-inch distance. That evening, Sally Sievert received a request to perform a repeat chest x-ray on Ms. Ampere.

Sally positioned the portable x-ray machine at the foot of Ms. Ampere's bed. She extended her arms between the patient's chest and the x-ray tube for 72-inch distance. Unfortunately, Sally Sievert's arms, when extended, measure only 53 inches. Sally Sievert used the same radiographic exposure settings indicated by Richard Rem. Due to the inconsistency in the source to image receptor distance brought about by the defective indicator ruler, Sally Sievert's radiograph of Ms. Ampere's chest was overexposed and not diagnostic due to the increased magnification of the heart. Sally had to repeat the radiograph, causing the patient, Ms. Ampere, additional radiation.

What are the legal risks involved in this situation?

ANSWER

One important duty of a radiographer is to ascertain that the equipment used in procedures and treatments is free from defects. The equipment must be appropriate for the purpose for which it is to be used. There are two elements to be considered for this particular duty. First, reasonably prudent care must be exercised in selecting equipment for a specific purpose. Second, reasonably prudent care must be exercised in the maintenance of the equipment. If the manufacturer's instructions require periodic inspections or other requirements to ensure optimum functioning, such instructions should be followed. If the radiographer observes that equipment is not functioning properly, the prudent action is to have it corrected by the individual responsible for its functioning at optimum level. The responsibility factor depends on several things: the situation itself, size of the hospital or medical center, number of staff radiographers available, and comparable components. If the radiographer is responsible, in any way, for the equipment functioning properly, it is wise to have documentation of the times the equipment is checked and found to be working properly, or if defects are found, that defects are corrected, when they are corrected, and by whom. There can be liability imposed on the radiographer and the hospital if equipment, facilities, and health systems fail to function properly. This does not mean the healthcare center must have the latest or the most expensive equipment. However, what it does have must be free from defects, operating at optimum capacity, and used by personnel who have been trained to use the equipment if special training is necessary.

REVIEW QUESTIONS

1. The legal doctrine that implies that every radiographer is liable for his/her conduct is:

    a.   Respondeat Superior.

    b.   Personal Liability.

    c.   Borrowed Servant.

    d.   Res Ipsa Loquitur.

2. Physicians are concerned about malpractice litigation be-
    cause the courts can hold them liable for:

    a.   Their own acts.

    b.   Their employees' acts.

    c.   The hospital's acts.

    d.   Both a and b.

    e.   All of the above.

3. If a radiographer were found to commit a negligent act, the
    court, under proper circumstances, could find the _____
    liable for negligence.

    a.   Radiographer.

    b.   Hospital/clinic.

    c.   Supervising physician.

    d.   All of the above.

    e.   Both b and c.

4. The fact that a radiographer follows hospital policy, but that
    the policy was found by the court to be in itself a negligent
    one, would probably result in the radiographer being re-
    garded by the court as acting:

    a.   Within the general standard of care.

    b.   Within the local standard of care.

    c.   Within the hospital's standard of care.

    d.   Negligently.

5. According to the *Simpson* v. *Sisters of Charity of Providence in
    Oregon* case, the radiographers were:

a.   Negligent because they did not meet the standard of care.

b.   Held personally liable for their negligence.

c.   Held not negligent because it is the duty of physicians to make final decisions as to the adequacy of films.

d.   Both a and b.

6. According to the *Barber* v. *St. Francis Cabrini Hospital* case, the court found that the patient's burn was the result of negligence by the:

a.   Radiographers.

b.   Hospital employees.

c.   Physician.

d.   All of the above.

7. The legal doctrine that is referred to as the "Captain of the Ship" doctrine is termed:

a.   Respondeat Superior.

b.   Personal Liability.

c.   Borrowed Servant.

d.   Res Ipsa Loquitur.

CHAPTER THREE

ANATOMY OF
A MALPRACTICE TRIAL

Upon completion of Chapter 3, the reader will be able to:

1. Discuss the concepts of a trial procedure.

2. Report on the function of the jury.

3. Identify the types of evidence that can be introduced to the court.

4. Define subpoena and subpoena duces tecum.

5. Construct a trial sequence.

6. Discuss proper courtroom protocol.

A civil suit begins with the filing of a petition or complaint in the court that has jurisdiction over the parties. Usually a sheriff delivers the complaint to the defendant, who must file an answer with the court responding to each allegation within the time specified, generally 21 days.

If you receive a complaint (a summons naming you as a defendant), your first step is to contact your professional insurer. The insurer will assign an attorney to investigate and defend the suit. If other parties with conflicting interests are named, e.g., physicians, each will have a different attorney.

After the complaints have been filed with the court and the defendants have been notified, the suit enters the discovery phase—a preliminary fact-finding stage that helps the attorneys narrow down the legal issues and expand the liability and defense theories. During discovery, before the deposition is taken, each party submits interrogatories, a series of written questions that must be answered under oath. The plaintiff, for instance, may ask the defendant radiographer the name of the radiologist who supervises his/her radiological activities. The defendant may ask the plaintiff the names and addresses of all physicians, including the radiologist who treated him/her over the past five years.

A *deposition* is oral testimony—transcribed as it is given—made under oath in the presence of all attorneys involved in the suit. The main purpose of taking depositions is to uncover information and establish a record that may be used to the advantage of either party at the trial. A secondary purpose may be to size up the witnesses and determine whether they would be effective before a jury.

Depositions are expensive and time consuming to prepare and therefore are not done unless the attorney believes important information will be obtained. The deponent, one who gives written testimony under oath, may be a party to the suit, a nonparty, or an expert.

The deposition usually begins with questions from the attorney who requested it; then the deponent's attorney will cross-examine his/her own client to clarify the record or minimize any harm that may have developed from the testimony. Other attorneys present will also do a cross-examination to protect the interests of their clients.

A person who is being deposed must be as well prepared for the deposition as is a witness who is going to testify in court. No one should approach a deposition without in-depth preparation. If you are named defendant, you need to review the hospital records on the case and discuss with your attorney the scope, objectives, and pitfalls inherent in a deposition. Sometimes it helps to read an old transcript to understand the process so that you will feel comfortable answering the questions. If time permits, you may want to sit in on a trial to hear actual testimony.

Respond simply and directly to all questions, but do not answer any question unless you understand what is being asked. Insist that the attorney be clear. When necessary, ask that the question be repeated or clarified.

During the trial, the deposition may be used in several ways:

1. If the defendant has made an admission, that part of the transcript may be read to the jury even though the defendant is on the witness stand.

2. The deposition may be used to "impeach" the credibility of the witness at the trial, i.e., to show the witness said one thing at the time of the deposition and something different at the trial.

During the deposition, *exhibits* will be introduced and made a part of the transcript. Exhibits include materials such as a hospital policy manual, radiology records, radiographs, radiographic accessory equipment that can be carried into court, and IV syringes, needles, and material.

Preparation is the key word in giving a good deposition. You must have a good handle on the facts involved, but avoid trying to impress the attorney with your command of scientific knowledge or trying to outsmart the opponent's attorney. The lawyers need your expertise, and you can rely on theirs.[1]

TRIAL PROCEDURE

The courtroom can be a tedious, as well as tempestuous, scene. Each of the main actors in the courtroom drama has a distinct role to perform. The initiator of the suit is the *plaintiff.* The one against whom the suit is brought is the *defendant.* In a civil suit, the case is captioned "Joe Plaintiff v. Sam Defendant." A lawsuit is formally initiated by filing a complaint against the defendant. It is then necessary for the defendant to respond promptly to the complaint.

Each party presents its evidence through its attorney. Litigation is civilized, legalized warfare. It is incumbent upon the attorneys to represent their client's best interest using every argument, technique, and legitimate procedural device to achieve that end.

In many cases, a settlement is made before any formal legal action takes place. If pretrial settlement negotiations are successful, the claim is settled. A general release is then signed by the plaintiff surrendering the right of any further action against the defendant.

Radiographers are becoming more involved in giving testimony in various cases. It is necessary, therefore, to be aware of one's accountability in these settings. Radiographers, like other citizens, are subject to a summons or subpoena ordering them to testify as a witness to a particular event. Situations in which a radiographer can be called to testify in a professional capacity are grievance procedures, malpractice cases (as an expert witness), and attesting to legal documents such as a radiograph or x-ray requisition.

The purpose of the court is to find out the truth concerning matters with evidence presented before the court and to apply the law to such matters. The function of the judge is to:

1. Ensure that the trial is conducted properly.

2. Strive for an atmosphere of impartiality.

3. Refrain from any act, word, sign, gesture, or inflection of voice that would affect any predisposition toward one side or the other.

4. Question any witness to clarify matters.

5. Not influence the jury.

Everyone has the constitutional right of trial by jury. Trial by jury applies to cases of *common law* and *statutory law*. A jury trial *CANNOT* be held in

1. Probate court, unless expressed by statute;

2. Cases in equity;

3. Civil cases in admiralty or maritime jurisdiction;

4. Juvenile court;

5. Paternity proceedings; and

6. Cases in which there is no indictment.

Jury Function

In a case of negligence or breach of duty, a jury has a two-step analysis to make. It must determine whether such conduct was negligent. Once the conclusion of facts is made, then the jury must determine if conduct was negligent based on that same set of facts.

If the jury finds there has been liability on the part of the defendant, the jury must determine the amount of money to be given to the plaintiff to compensate him/her for his/her monetary losses, pain, and suffering. The plaintiff is entitled to be reimbursed for his/her medical expenses. He/she is entitled to the full amount in money damages of any economic loss, both present and future, as a result of the defendant's negligence. The plaintiff is said to be indemnified or "made whole again" (Hemelt & Mackert, 1982, p. 18).

Evidence

The law of evidence is the system of rules and standards by which the admission of proof at the trial of a lawsuit is regulated. Under the usual order of trial procedure, the plaintiff, who has the burden of proof or of establishing his/her claim, will introduce his/her evidence to prove the facts to establish his/her case. The plaintiff presents his/her version of the facts through witnesses and documents.

The law of evidence is a development of the common law. In our adversarial system, in order to assure that the triers of the facts receive only reliable information, comprehensive codes of evidence have been adopted. One method of presenting evidence to the court is by testimony of witnesses. Evidence must be identified before it is accepted as real evidence; therefore, it must be given under oath. Generally, all witnesses are sworn in before presenting testimony. Evidence can be of testimony, documents, objects, and admissions. There are three types of evidence:

1. Direct evidence, which is the testimony of witnesses.

2. Indirect or circumstantial evidence, testimony of witnesses from which certain conclusions and other facts are arrived at by *inference.*

3. Real or demonstrative evidence, presentation of objects to which the testimony refers. This evidence is for personal observation by the court or jury.

Subpoena

A subpoena is a court order commanding the person on whom it is served to appear at a given time and place to testify. A subpoena may be served by judges, the clerk of the court, attorneys and arbitrators, various boards and commissions of legislatures, and legislative committees. A subpoena is *valid* only within the state that has issued the subpoena. A subpoena has no extraterritorial effects. Willful disregard of a subpoena is punishable as a *Contempt of the Court.*

Subpoena Duces Tecum—Subpoena of Record

A subpoena duces tecum is a command for the witness to bring with him/her the appropriate documents, papers, or books noted in the subpoena. A subpoena duces tecum can imply medical records, consents and/or authorizations, reports, radiographic reports, and radiographs.

Trial Sequence

The opening statement is made by the plaintiff's counsel followed by an opening statement by the defense counsel. Both outline what they intend to prove.

The plaintiff presents his case with testimony, exhibits, and other evidence to prove and support the allegations or claims. The defense moves for a directed verdict upon the close of the plaintiff's case, and argues that the plaintiff has not made out a sufficient case and that all charges should be dismissed. If directed verdict is denied, the defense moves forward with the rebuttal, presenting testimony, exhibits, and other evidence to negate and deny the plaintiff's allegations.

Concluding arguments are made by both counsels to the jury. The trial judge instructs the jury on the law related to the case. The jury retires to make a decision.

Right of Appeal

A party against whom an adverse decision is rendered may wish to appeal to a higher court. An appellate court does not re-try a case and hear all the evidence again. The appellate court considers primarily errors in the law. The basic distinction is that an appellate court generally sits to review the question of law—not the question of fact. It must be emphasized that an appeal will not overturn findings of fact made by a judge or jury, based on evaluation of all the testimony and evidence, unless the findings are clearly erroneous.

Courtroom Protocol

One thing that remains a constant is that the success or failure of an entire case can depend on any one witness. Therefore, the witness's attitude, demeanor, and appearance are critical toward winning the case. Juries are easily alienated by such tactics. Good manners are expected as a matter of course in the courtroom by witnesses and attorneys alike.

Credibility is inherent in the truthfulness of the statements made. However, there are some techniques that can be used to enhance one's credibility. Certain basic things should be done by all witnesses. The following are considered fundamental to a witness who wishes to make an appropriate impression on the jury:

1. Dress neatly and conservatively. The jury is receiving a composite picture of the witness.

2. Listen carefully to the questions asked. Answer the questions clearly and calmly, and speak in a firm and audible tone. By speaking slowly, you give the attorney the opportunity to object in a timely fashion. Do not expand your

answers, do not volunteer any information, and do not hesitate to say, " I don't know" or " I don't remember."

3. Generally, all witnesses are treated politely by counsel, but if an attorney is rude or arrogant with you, don't respond with rudeness or by losing your temper. Remain courteous and polite at all times.

4. Review any relevant documents, reports, and records prior to trial or deposition to refresh your memory. Tell the truth as you perceive the truth and relate the facts of the case. Try not to testify about what someone else said or did unless asked. This is considered hearsay evidence.

5. It is the attorney's job to protect the client and the witnesses for the client. Don't confuse your role as a witness and try to become the advocate for the client's cause.

6. A classic question often asked of the witness is, "Have you discussed this case with anyone?" The answer is generally "yes" since you have discussed it with the attorney, possibly the insurance company representative, and any other appropriate parties. It is expected procedure.

7. If an objection is made, don't continue to answer the question. Wait for the attorney to re-question following the objection.

VIGNETTE 7—NEW TRIAL FOR PATIENT'S SUIT AGAINST SURGEON

A patient was entitled to a new trial of a malpractice claim against a surgeon who allegedly left a wire in her body, a North Carolina appellate court ruled.

On October 6, 1975, the surgeon performed a laparotomy on the patient. Because of the poor condition of her veins at the time of surgery, the surgeon had to perform a cutdown in order to insert an intravenous catheter. The patient alleged that the catheter contained a thin stainless steel wire that was left in her body after the catheter was removed. The physician denied that the IV line that he inserted contained such a wire. Before the laparotomy, the patient had undergone other cutdowns by other surgeons and later during her illness several catheters were inserted for IV purposes.

After the operation by the surgeon, the patient complained of chest and abdominal pains. She was hospitalized in November and December 1975. In April 1976, she began to experience abdominal swelling. In May 1976, the surgeon performed a second operation in which he removed an 8 1/2-inch steel wire that was embedded in her liver.

The incision created by the second operation did not heal properly, and in February 1978, she underwent surgery to remove scarring or adhesions in her abdominal cavity conceivably related to the May 1976 surgery.

As a result of her medical problems, she was unable to work. She lost weight and could not function effectively at home, and her husband had incurred medical bills totalling $43,000. In a malpractice action against the surgeon, a trial court entered a judgment for the physician.

Ordering a new trial, the appellate court concluded that the presence of an 8 1/2-inch wire embedded in the patient's liver, allegedly there as a result of a cutdown by a surgeon, was so inconsistent with the exercise of due care as to raise an inference of lack of care (*The Citation*, 44(9), February 15, 1982).

What legal doctrine(s) apply to this case? Who, if anyone, would be held liable in this case?

ANSWER

The appellate court held that there was legally sufficient evidence to establish the law of *res ipsa loquitur* and that the physician failed to meet the standard of care required of physicians in similar circumstances and that as a direct consequence, the patient sustained injuries and unnecessary surgery. The physician would be directly liable in this case.

ENDNOTE

1. Excerpts from Cushing, M. 1985. How a suit starts. *American Journal of Nursing, 85*(6), 655–656.

REVIEW QUESTIONS

1. If a radiographer receives a summons naming him/her as a defendant, the first step is to:

    a.   Quit the job.

    b.   Notify the administrator.

    c.   Notify the State Radiologic Health Branch–Certification.

    d.   Contact the professional insurance company.

2. A series of written questions that must be answered under oath is called:

    a.   Interrogatory.

    b.   Deposition.

    c.   Subpoena.

    d.   Testimony.

3. A deposition is _____ testimony.

    a.   Oral.

    b.   Written.

4. The deposition may be used to _____ the credibility of the witness at the trial.

    a.   Clarify.

    b.   Impeach.

    c.   Minimize.

5. The initiator of a suit is called the:

    a.   Defendant.

    b.   Judge.

    c.   Plaintiff.

    d.   Attorney.

6. In a trial case, who determines the amount of money to be given to a plaintiff to compensate for monetary losses, pain, and suffering?

    a.   Jury.

    b.   Judge.

    c.   District attorney.

    d.   None of the above.

7. A court order commanding a person to appear at a given time and place to testify is:

    a.   Deposition.

    b.   Interrogatory.

    c.   Subpoena.

    d.   Evidence.

8. The appellate court will consider primarily errors in the:

    a.   Evidence submitted.

    b.   Law.

    c.   Attorney's deposition.

    d.   None of the above.

CHAPTER FOUR

HOSPITAL LABOR RELATIONS

Upon completion of Chapter 4, the reader will be able to:

1. Recognize the importance of employee/employer hiring contracts.

2. Examine the integrity of organized labor unions.

3. Apply the regulations of the Fair Labor Practices Act and the Equal Pay Act to employer contracts.

4. Interpret the regulations of the Occupational Safety and Health Act.

5. Recall the forms of offensive behavior that are listed in the Equal Employment Opportunity Act.

6. Report on the state laws concerning labor and explain the State Fair Employment Act, Anti-Injunction Act, and the Worker's Compensation Act.

Hospitals differ from industrial enterprises in their financial and social contracts. Most of the hospitals in the United States are categorized as government owned, corporate owned, or voluntary nonprofit associations.

MASTER-SERVANT RELATIONSHIP. An employee is a servant engaged to render a service to another. While that person renders such service personally, he remains under the *control* and *direction* of the employer. The employer is designated as the "Master."

Radiology administrators constantly find themselves in situations that demand quick and confident action. Radiology administrators are called on to make decisions and take action that involves some legal standing and could cost the hospital or medical center big money.

A $7 million lawsuit was filed by an employee who claimed he was illegally fired by the radiology administrator. The disgruntled employee grossed a small fortune the new American way—through the courts. As employees resolve more and more of their grievances before the courts, all kinds of people benefit. Once attorneys find out they can make money on a particular type of case, it becomes very popular.

EMPLOYER CONTRACTS

The employment contract begins with an understanding between employer and employee at the time of the initial interview prior to actual job performance. When the radiographer accepts a job at a particular institution, hospital, clinic, or private physician's office, he/she has entered into a *contract.* There is the basic understanding that the radiographer will perform the job competently, safely, and in accordance with the standards and policies of the institution. More importantly, there is an understanding that the institution will *pay* for those services, will provide the certified radiographic/fluoroscopic equipment to perform those services, and will maintain the facilities and equipment in a proper manner to encourage efficiency and competency in job performance. There is a mutual obligation on the part of both employer and employee arising from the work contract. Many institutions *do not* have written contracts. Instead, they have a general understanding at the time of employment and prefer to have the policy statements serve as a basis for contractual obligations. Although this could be considered *poor business* practice on the part of both the employer and employee, the courts could still construe a contract from the circumstances under which both parties were working. It is much easier to interpret a written contract of employment than it is to interpret the oral understanding of two parties that may have occurred five or ten years previously.

Often the issue arises where a sonographer alleges he/she was hired with the clear understanding that he/she would perform only diagnostic sonography examinations or would have every other weekend off. Subsequently, new rules and policies are established or a new administrator comes to the institution. Under the new situation, the sonographer is told that he/she must also perform diagnostic radiographic/fluoroscopic examinations or that he/she will have only one weekend off a month. Before the sonographer could be successful in establishing a breach of contract against the employer, the sonographer must show that there was a mutual understanding of the original particular facts, as well as all the other elements of a contract. There must be *proof* of the existence of such a contract. How much easier it would be for the sonographer to insist that the conditions of the contract be met if he/she has a statement in *writing* to the effect that he/she was hired to work in sonography with every other weekend off. How difficult it is to prove anything where the parties have only their memories, with conflicting interpretations of what took place at the initial interview. This does not mean that the law will not enforce a verbal contract. The emphasis is on the difficulty of proving what actually took place.

When the employee claims he/she was hired to do a specific job and was to have certain weekends off but lacks written documentation, he/she does not necessarily lose the case. The courts will generally apply the standard of reasonableness to the situation. In conjunction with the evidence presented by both parties, where certain points are vague, indefinite, or controverted, the courts determine what could reasonably be expected to occur and generally construe the contract in that light unless there is substantive evidence to the contrary.

The question of employment expectations/requirements sometimes arises from radiology administrators or directors of human resources if they are responsible for checking the applicant's credentials, including licensure, registry, graduation, and relevant job qualifications. For example, suppose if after hiring an individual it was discovered that he/she had a drug problem or that he/she had stolen someone else's license/registry and was not even a licensed/registered radiographer as purported. It is unfortunate that this and similar situations do occur. However, the legal obligation of radiology administrators, personnel directors, and those in similar positions is to make reasonable inquiries regarding the credentials of the individual applicant. The law does not place a burden of doing a full investigation on every applicant for a position. Under ordinary circumstances, there is a right to presume that the applicant's credentials are bona fide. Unless there are circumstances which would lead a reasonably prudent person to suspect that the applicant may be a fraud or may be incompetent, personnel directors and administrators have the right to assume that they are dealing with a credible individual. Most healthcare institutions, like most businesses, have a protocol to follow for reviewing credentials and getting references. If the protocol is followed and is a comparable procedure to similar healthcare institutions, then the expectations of the law would generally have been met.

It is good business practice to have the various terms of the contract, such as hours, days off, salary, vacation time, and any unusual arrangements, as specific as possible. Whenever possible, make the commitment in writing, with a memorandum of understanding attached if necessary. Otherwise, the court may have to interpret any ambiguities. A hiring contract should list:

1. Pay scales.

2. Sick leave policy.

3. Paid vacation period.

4. The required period of work before vacation.

5. Holiday time off.

6. Work schedules.

7. Insurance benefits, including monetary value.

8. Liability insurance coverage (amount).

9. Discharge expectations—a 90-day probationary period for the employer and employee. Reasonable notice to terminate must be given to the employer and include an exit interview by the personnel director.

VIGNETTE 8—STAFFING

Ronny Rad, R.T., was hired to work as a computerized tomography technologist in the radiology department at Los Altos Medical Center. On Tuesday morning, Ronny Rad arrived in the department at 8:00 A.M., according to department routine. Bill Roentgen, radiology department administrator, told Ronny Rad that it would be necessary for Ronny to perform fluoroscopic examinations due to the radiology department being understaffed in the diagnostic area and a decrease in patient examinations in the computerized tomography area.

Ronny Rad informed Bill Roentgen that he had not worked in the diagnostic area performing fluoroscopic examinations in 15 years, that he was unfamiliar with the routine procedures, and that he could not perform quality radiographs for diagnostic interpretation.

What, if any, are the legal risks for Ronny Rad and Bill Roentgen under these circumstances?

ANSWER

The first issue to be considered is the hiring agreement between Ronny Rad and Bill Roentgen. Was Ronny hired specifically as a computerized tomography technologist with the understanding or written agreement that he would not be moved from area to area? If a determination of an implied or expressed understanding is made, or a written document demonstrating that Ronny Rad was hired specifically as a computerized tomography technologist is presented, then Ronny would be within his legal rights to refuse to perform fluoroscopic procedures.

At the same time, the radiography staff should not refuse to go to another area of the radiology department by saying they are incapable of performing radiographic procedures for the sake of not performing the examination. Computerized tomography technologists are basically licensed and registered radiographers; it would be unprofessional for Ronny Rad not to maintain his radiography skills in all areas of radiography.

More specifically, it would be appropriate for radiographers to be cross-trained and rotated through the various imaging modalities (i.e., CT scan, MRI, sonography). In this way, the radiography staff can learn new skills and be more efficient. It is the legal obligation of Bill Roentgen to ensure that the radiology department has adequate employee coverage for increases in patient examinations and/or shortages in staffing.

ORGANIZED LABOR UNIONS

Why do persons organize or join a union? The general reason given for joining a union is to increase employee power and to be certain of a response from management. The healthcare industry is behind in employee fringe benefits vs. the manufacturing industry. Other reasons for labor to organize are:

1. To correct any job inequities, such as advancement, pay increments, promotion, and benefits.

2. To provide the employee with job security, pension plans, and healthcare coverage.

The 1974 amendment to the *Taft-Hartley Act* established a procedure for elections and collective bargaining covering nonprofit and voluntary hospitals. This means that all healthcare workers, from aides to technologists to physicians and hospital administrators, have a right to be represented by a union in determining certain employment conditions. Through union representation and collective bargaining, the individual employee has a stronger voice and more leverage in seeking responses from the employer. By establishing a procedure for collective bargaining, Congress laid a foundation for orderly and civilized resolution of disputes in the healthcare arena.

With respect to collective bargaining, there are some people who think that there will be nothing but strikes and increased costs. The fact is that strikes are the exception. No one wants a strike. It is economically injurious for both sides of the negotiations. It is held in abeyance as a last resort. No one wants to suffer economic deprivation. That is what a strike means to both sides of the negotiating table. Employees will lose wages for the term of the strike, be forced to use their savings, and very often, even if they "win" the strike, the increase in wages does not make up for the lost income. Employers also are not productive during the term of the strike. Consequently, profits are decreased. Whether employers win or lose the strike issues, there is always an economic loss.

The *National Labor Relations Act* allows any group of employees the right to organize and represent the rights and interests of others, whether those employees are unionized or not.

UNFAIR LABOR PRACTICES

Healthcare facilities, such as hospitals and medical centers, are subject to the laws of the states that charter them. The *Labor Management Act* and the various state labor relations acts *prohibit* hospitals/medical centers from engaging in certain conduct classified as employer unfair labor relations. For example, prior to terminating an employee, there must be at least three written reports documenting any discrepancies in employment. The employee must be counselled and given an opportunity to improve these discrepancies.

FAIR LABOR STANDARDS ACT

The U.S. Department of Labor is concerned with the issue of wages and hours. The department closely monitors issues of overtime.

The *Fair Labor Standards Act* requires hospitals/medical centers to pay their employees at least minimum wage. In addition, hospitals/medical centers are required to compensate employees at a rate of 1.5 times the regular rate of pay for all hours worked in excess of an 8-hour day and/or a 40-hour week.

However, if the employer/employee hiring contract documents a bi-weekly pay period, then the 1.5 times the regular rate of pay will be paid for all hours worked in excess of 8 hours/day and/or 80 hours/pay period. THIS DOES NOT APPLY TO SALARIED OR CONTRACTED EMPLOYMENT.

Overtime is *not* mandatory. The employer must get the approval of the employee for extra work hours. Care must be taken to make sure that the radiographer does not leave the department or end the work shift if the radiographer is performing a patient procedure.

The *Equal Pay Act* demands that employees performing equal jobs be paid equally. Many hospitals are sued under this legislation. Medical aides and orderlies often perform the same job but may be paid differently. In one suit at a hospital, a disgruntled aide sued the facility because of such pay differences. The court found that orderlies indeed were paid more than aides. It also ruled that the pay scale was unfair, but not because the two groups performed the same duties. Instead, the judge found that orderlies actually did less work than the lower paid aides. Because the law states that equal effort must be rewarded with equal pay, the hospital was not violating the law. However, while the hospital was off the hook legally, it changed the pay scale to eliminate the inequity.

CIVIL RIGHTS ACT OF 1991

This statute provides that a denial of equal job opportunities on the basis of race, color, religion, sex, or national origin is *illegal.*

The *Occupational Safety and Health Act* (OSHA) protects employees from abuses of employers. OSHA inspectors are free to visit any department in a hospital. As a regulatory agency, OSHA strives to keep current with the times. For example, the agency has published regulations regarding blood-borne pathogens; its aim is to protect employees from being exposed to deadly viruses.

Many changes have been made in the Hazard Communication Standards, which require that employers who keep hazardous materials in the workplace must train and inform their employees on the dangers and precautions of the substances.

The hazardous communications regulations require employers to do the following:

1. Employers must have a written program stating what the company's overall policy is in handling hazardous chemicals and how they plan to protect employees.

2. All chemicals must be properly labelled and include information on the chemical's name, what hazard it presents, and where the employee can get more information.

3. Employee training must be provided. Training can be as elaborate as an audiovisual session or as simple as a consultation session with employees.

4. All chemicals must have material-safety data sheets containing this information.

Noncompliance with these standards could result in fines to the radiology department.

EQUAL EMPLOYMENT OPPORTUNITY ACT

Radiology administrators are not immune from the confusing and unwelcome issue of sexual harassment. Radiology administrators have a responsibility to act on sexual harassment claims immediately. The employer has the responsibility to eliminate the atmosphere in which harassment has been alleged. Complainants have the option of bringing the issue to the attention of the Equal Employment Opportunity Commission (EEOC), or they can go through the federal and state court system.

According to the EEOC, sexual harassment is defined as unwanted sexual advances, or visual, verbal or physical conduct of a sexual nature. While this definition includes many forms of offensive behavior, the following is a partial list:

1. Unwanted sexual advances.

2. Offering employment benefits in exchange for sexual favors.

3. Making or threatening reprisals after a negative response to sexual advances.

4. Visual conduct—leering, making sexual gestures, displaying of sexually suggestive objects or pictures, cartoons, or posters.

5. Verbal conduct—making or using derogatory comments, epithets, slurs, and jokes.

6. Verbal sexual advances or propositions.

7. Verbal abuse of a sexual nature, graphic verbal commentaries about an individual's body, sexually degrading words used to describe an individual, suggestive or obscene letters, notes, or invitations.

8. Physical conduct—touching, assault, impeding or blocking movement.

If harassment does occur, the employer may be liable even if management was not aware of the harassment. The employer may avoid liability when the harasser is a rank and file employee and there was a program to prevent harassment. The harasser, as well as any management representative who knew about the harassment and condoned or ratified it, can be held personally liable for damages. The employer must take all "reasonable" steps to prevent harassment from occurring. If the employer has failed to take such preventive measures, that employer can be held liable for the employee's harassment.

An act of harassment, by itself, is an unlawful act. A victim may be entitled to damages even though no employment opportunity has been denied and there is no actual loss of pay or benefits.

The three most common types of sexual harassment complaints filed with the commission are:

1. An employee is fired or denied a job or an employment benefit because he/she refused to grant sexual favors or because he/she complained about harassment. Retaliation for complaining about harassment is illegal, even if it cannot be demonstrated that the harassment actually occurred.

2. An employee quits because he/she can no longer tolerate an offensive work environment. This is referred to as a constructive discharge harassment case. If it is proven that a reasonable person, under like conditions, would resign to escape the harassment, the employer may be held responsible for the resignation as if the employee had been discharged.

3. An employee is exposed to an offensive work environment. Exposure to various kinds of behavior or to unwanted sexual advances alone may constitute harassment.

A program to eliminate sexual harassment from the workplace is not only good business, but it is the most practical way to avoid or limit damages if harassment should occur despite preventive efforts. The employer should take immediate and appropriate action when he/she knows, or should have known, that sexual harassment has occurred. An employer should take effective action to stop any further harassment and to ameliorate any effects of the harassment. To those ends, the employer's policy should include provisions to:

1. Fully inform a complainant of his/her rights and any obligations to secure those rights.

2. Fully and effectively investigate. It must be immediate, thorough, objective, and complete. All those with information on the matter should be interviewed. A determination should be made and the results communicated to the complainant, to the alleged harasser, and as appropriate, to all others directly concerned.

3. If proven, there should be prompt and effective remedial action. First, appropriate action should be taken against the harasser and communicated to the complainant. Second, steps should be taken to prevent any further harassment. Third, appropriate action should be taken to remedy the complainant's loss, if any.

All employees should be made aware of the seriousness of violations of the sexual harassment policy. Supervisory personnel should be educated about their specific responsibilities. Rank and file employees should be cautioned against using peer pressure to discourage harassment victims from using the internal grievance procedure.

VIGNETTE 9—SEXUAL HARASSMENT

Rosy Rem, R.T., is a staff radiographer at Phantom Medical Center. Rosy Rem had complained to her supervisor, Bonnie Blur, R.T., that the radiologist, Donald Diode, M.D., has been sexually harassing her. Rosy Rem had indicated that Doctor Diode has been telling sexually oriented jokes around her and other staff members. Rosy Rem also reported that Doctor Diode has been making comments to her that were offensive.

More specifically, Rosy Rem's technical performance became increasingly poor every time she was assisting Doctor Diode with a radiographic procedure. Rosy Rem had told Bonnie Blur that she had told Doctor Diode she did not want him to tell any sexually oriented jokes in her presence. In addition, Rosy Rem informed Doctor Diode to stop making offensive sexual comments to her. Doctor Diode ignored Rosy Rem's objection and continued to make offensive comments in her presence.

Bonnie Blur, the supervising radiographer, had confronted Doctor Diode about Rosy Rem's verbal accusations of sexual harassment. Bonnie Blur instructed Doctor Diode to stop telling sexually oriented jokes and making sexually offensive comments in the presence of Rosy Rem. During this conversation, Doctor Diode claimed that Rosy Rem's technical abilities were less than satisfactory, and he insisted that Rosy Rem be terminated from the radiology department at Phantom Medical Center. Within a week, Rosy Rem was dismissed from the facility due to her poor technical skills. Bonnie Blur did not provide the Director of Human Resources, Clay Caliper, any written documentation of Rosy Rem's accusations of sexual harassment by Doctor Diode.

What would be Rosy Rem's legal recourse, if any?

ANSWER

Rosy Rem had done right by notifying her supervisor, Bonnie Blur, of the sexual harassment from Doctor Diode. Bonnie Blur should have taken immediate and appropriate action to stop any further harassment and to improve any effects of the harassment. Rosy Rem should not have been assigned to assist Doctor Diode until Bonnie Blur notified, in writing, the Director of Human Resources, Clay Caliper, of the sexual harassment complaint by Rosy Rem.

Clay Caliper should have immediately interviewed all parties involved with the incident. Steps should have been taken to prevent any further harassment and action should have been taken to remedy Rosy Rem's complaint.

Since Rosy Rem's poor technical skills may have been due to the mental anxiety of working with Doctor Diode, there may also be a case for wrongful termination. It is evident that Bonnie Blur did not manage this discrimination complaint effectively and within the guidelines of the Equal Employment Opportunity Act.

SAMPLE CASE: X-RAY TECHNICIAN SHOULD NOT HAVE BEEN TERMINATED BY HOSPITAL FOR PREGNANCY

A hospital's possible liability for x-ray exposure to a pregnant x-ray technician *did not* provide a "business necessity" for terminating the employment of the technician, a federal trial court in Alabama ruled.

The technician sued the hospital, claiming violations of the *Civil Rights Act.* The hospital contended that termination of the technician's employment was a business necessity and that nonpregnancy was a bona fide occupational qualification for operation of its enterprise.

The court found that the technician's pregnancy did not undermine her ability to take x-rays of patients. Even if the concept of a purpose of safe and efficient operation of the business was extended to include avoidance of possible litigation and potential liability to the fetus, the court said, the hospital did not meet the requirement of the business necessity defense that there were no acceptable alternatives.

Evidence revealed that prior to the technician's termination, two pregnant, white radiology technicians were *not* fired but that greater precautions were taken, and one was allowed to *read* x-ray films during her pregnancy. The court found that the hospital failed to show that no alternatives to its discriminatory treatment of the technician were available.

As to the bona fide occupational qualification defense, the court said that the hospital must show a connection between pregnancy risks and impaired ability to perform the job. The court found that pregnancy would not have affected the technician's performance as a radiologist and, therefore, the hospital could not rely on that defense.

The court held that the hospital's abrupt termination of the technician's employment constituted a violation of the Civil Rights Act and awarded her $7,361.76 as damages (*Hayes* v. *Shelby Memorial Hospital,* 546 F. Supp.

259 DC, Alabama, August 18, 1983, in *The Citation*, 46(8), 1983, American Medical Association).

STATE LAWS CONCERNING LABOR

Most states will model their labor laws after the *National Labor Relations Act*, also known as the *Wagner Act*.

State Fair Employment Practice Act

It is unlawful for any employer, employment agency, or labor organization to discriminate in hiring, discharge, compensation, and conditions of employment on the basis of race, creed, color, or national origin of any individual. Should discrimination be alleged, a complaint may be filed by the injured party or the state attorney general's office.

SAMPLE CASE: FIRED WORKER CAN SUE "UNDER-STAFFED" HOSPITAL

The state supreme court allowed a hospital worker in Orange County to sue over her firing which followed her refusal to work a night shift that she said was dangerously understaffed.

The court unanimously denied a hearing on an appeal by Gail Dabbs' employer from an appellate ruling allowing her to seek damages on a claim that her firing violated a public policy to protect patients from harm.

The ruling by the Fourth District Court of Appeals in Santa Ana was strongly protested by the hospital, which said the court's analysis would convert "uncooperative, lazy, or arrogant employees" into "heroic guardians of patient safety."

The supreme court's action makes the ruling binding on trial courts statewide.

Dabbs, 50, of Laguna Beach, is a certified respiratory therapist who was working for San Clemente General Hospital in 1983. She said her unit was supposed to have three qualified therapists for intensive care patients on the 3:00 P.M. to 11:00 P.M. shift, but on the night in question, there was only one other therapist who was new and unqualified.

After officials refused to provide another qualified therapist, Dabbs said, she refused to work and was fired. She now works for a healthcare facility in Tustin.

Orange County Superior Court Judge Judith Ryan dismissed Dabbs' suit for lost wages and emotional distress, saying she would have broken no law working in an understaffed ward and could not sue on the grounds of general public policy. But the appeals court reinstated the suit. "California has a public policy favoring qualified care for its ill and infirm," said the opinion by presiding Justice John Trotter. He said society's concern for patient care protects health workers from being fired for voicing dissatisfaction with procedures they reasonably believe will endanger patients in their care (*The Orange County Register*, April 1987, p. A-3).

State Anti-Injunction Act (Norris-LaGuardia Act)

An *injunction* is a court order to protect labor from abuses of restraining orders from industry. This usually applies during labor strikes. For example, there may be a danger to sick patients who may be deprived of vital services should hospital employees strike. A preliminary injunction order may be issued restraining the strikers from interfering with the orderly operation of the hospital.

State Worker's Compensation Statute

Worker's compensation laws provide for the payment of compensation and medical benefits to a person who is injured as the result of an industrial accident, an occupational disease, and to the dependents of the worker in the case of death. Worker's compensation benefits are paid to the worker even though the worker may have contributed to the negligent act.

An employee who is injured while performing job-related duties may sue the employer for injuries suffered. Worker's compensation laws give the employee a legal way to receive compensation for injuries on the job. The acts do not require the employee to prove that the injury was the result of the employer's negligence. Worker's compensation laws are based on the employer/employee relationship and not upon the theory of negligence (Pozgar, 1987, p. 176).

VIGNETTE 10—WORKER'S COMPENSATION CASE

Barbara Barium, R.T., was lifting a patient onto the x-ray table from the stretcher. Ms. Barium felt something snap in her back and a pain shoot down her left leg. She continued to work although she was in severe pain. The radiology department supervisor advised Ms. Barium to go to the health clinic to be examined. Following a visit to the health clinic, x-rays of Barbara Barium's back were taken. The x-rays revealed a herniated lumbar intervertebral disc between the fourth and fifth lumbar vertebra. There were no arthritic, degenerative disc changes.

Barbara Barium filed a workman's compensation claim alleging the above facts and claiming that she was injured in the line of duty. The employer-hospital denied the allegations, stating there was a prior injury that caused the plaintiff's backache and disability. The hospital also argued the registered radiographer should have sought help in moving the patient. Even if the radiographer did injure herself as she alleged, it could have been prevented by acting as a reasonably prudent radiographer and seeking assistance.

What decision should be made in this case and why?

ANSWER

The facts of the case show that Barbara Barium was injured while on duty and while caring for a patient. The key test is that the injuries arose out of, and in the course of, her employment. Radiographer Barbara Barium followed appropriate procedure and hospital policy following the injury. She dutifully reported the injury and underwent examination and x-rays.

The purpose of worker's compensation insurance is to protect workers who are injured on the job. It is not a question of assigning negligence or assessing wrongdoing. Worker's compensation benefits should be awarded to the radiographer or any other employee injured in the course of their employment. It is imperative that when you are injured while on duty, you should always

1. report the injury to the radiology department supervisor or hospital nursing supervisor,

2. document the incident by filing an incident report, and

3. go the health clinic or hospital emergency room department for an examination by a physician.

REVIEW QUESTIONS

1. A general unwritten understanding at the time of employment is:

    a. Acceptable.

    b. Unlawful.

    c. Unacceptable.

    d. Poor business practice.

2. When a radiographer claims to have been hired to do a specific job but lacks written confirmation, the court may apply a standard of _____ to the situation.

    a. Law.

    b. Reasonableness.

    c. Evidence.

    d. Care.

3. Checking the radiographer's credentials, licensure, registry, and job qualifications is the responsibility of the:

   a.   Employer.

   b.   Radiologist.

   c.   Chief radiographer.

   d.   All of the above.

4. A proper written employment contract should have the following terms listed except the:

   a.   Paid vacation period.

   b.   Liability insurance.

   c.   Work schedule.

   d.   Radiographic techniques.

5. There is usually a _____-day probationary period for new employees.

   a.   90.

   b.   60.

   c.   30.

   d.   10.

6. It would be _____ for a radiographer to refuse to perform a radiographic examination.

   a.   Illegal.

   b.   Unethical.

   c.   Acceptable.

   d.   Unacceptable.

7. It is the legal obligation of the _____ to ensure that the radiology department has adequate employee coverage.

    a.   Hospital administrator.

    b.   Radiologist.

    c.   Chief radiographer.

    d.   Personnel director.

8. The federal statute that establishes procedures for collective bargaining is the:

    a.   Norris-LaGuardia Act.

    b.   Fair Labor Standards Act.

    c.   Taft-Hartley Act.

    d.   Civil Rights Act.

9. The federal statute that requires employers to compensate employees at 1.5 times the regular rate of pay for all hours worked in excess of 8 hours/day, 40 hours/week is the:

    a.   Norris-LaGuardia Act.

    b.   Fair Labor Standards Act.

    c.   Taft-Hartley Act.

    d.   Civil Rights Act.

10. A court order prohibiting strikes from interfering with the orderly operation of the hospital is called:

    a.   Injunction.

    b.   Restraining order.

    c.   Compensation.

    d.   None of the above.

11. The federal law that protects workers from hazardous working conditions is the:

    a.   Equal Employment Opportunity Act.

    b.   Equal Pay Act.

    c.   Occupational Safety and Health Act.

    d.   Department of Labor Hazardous Work Act.

12. The federal law that ensures that candidates are not discriminated against based on a wide set of criteria is the:

    a.   Equal Employment Opportunity Act.

    b.   Equal Pay Act.

    c.   Occupational Safety and Health Act.

    d.   1991 Civil Rights Act.

CHAPTER FIVE

RISK MANAGEMENT AND LIABILITY

Upon completion of Chapter 5, the reader will be able to:

1. Define liability.

2. Apply the Doctrine of Corporate Negligence to the case of *Darling* v. *Charleston Community Hospital.*

3. Recognize the responsibility of the professional staff regarding liability.

4. Discuss the Good Samaritan Laws.

5. Explain hospital liability and malpractice.

6. Assess the importance of patient injury reporting and recording.

The physician opens the lead-lined door and steps onto the brightly lit hallway. The act and its required effort were harder this time—it always is when one must face the family.

In the waiting room, she sees that the hospital chaplain has arrived. A quick glance before turning to the parents. Their faces are ashen, yet it's their eyes she hates the most. For without saying a word, the dire nonverbal messages had been conveyed. "No your daughter is not dead," the doctor says. "During the examination, however, she experienced complications. She is now in a coma."

What? How? Why? These are questions that demand answers, questions that will be answered with compassion. Both the questions and the answers will never end. "She had a seizure and went into cardiac arrest," the physician explains. "We got her back, and now hope that she'll respond further. You may see her for a few minutes. She is on a machine that assists her breathing. We're doing everything we can."

The kidney exam was necessary. Her right lower quadrant pain and work-up tests confirmed it. The IV was established. The questionnaire was completed. The patient's history of hayfever and asthma, as well as the evening hour, called for non-ionic contrast. The risks were known. Radiology personnel were ready for everything—except the physician's response time.

The injection went smoothly. Following the initial film, the young female patient and the radiographer were talking about the previous night's awards show. Then the grand mal hit. Its intensity peaked so rapidly that the radiographer had to grab the girl to keep her from throwing herself off the table. The reaction tray was nearby, but the telephone was ten feet away.

"The emergency room is just down the hall," thought the radiographer. "And the ordering emergency room physician knows where we are."

The patient's strength was overwhelming. Her gurgled sounds grew worse in the radiographer's ear. The radiographer's calls for help were smothered by the enclosed room.

Then the tremors ceased as quickly as they had begun, to be replaced by stillness and quiet. The radiographer raced to the telephone, dialing the code.

Time seemed frozen or in slow motion. How much time had elapsed? Where were they?

Finally the sounds of the team approached. Were they called soon enough?[1]

This story, although fictitious, is a concern for many radiographers who are performing radiographic procedures without direct or immediate supervision from the physician. Hospital policy should dictate that the ordering physician or radiologist be present during the injection of contrast media and remain to monitor the patient for ten minutes. The physician could then return if complications arise.

An acute care hospital/medical center is under the duty to exercise such reasonable care in looking after and protecting the patient. The legal responsibility of any health practitioner is to be a practitioner of safe care. The following legal doctrine will provide insight into the ways in which the law fixes liability for acts of malpractice. Radiographers may be subjected to a greater exposure of liability based upon various factors, or principles of law, or legal status of the employer or the employee.

Risk management is the process of avoiding or controlling risk of financial loss to the radiographers and the hospital or medical center. Risk management is a matter of patient safety. Poor quality care will create a risk of injury to patients and will lead to increased financial liability. Risk management is engaged in the protection of financial assets by managing insurance for potential liability by reducing liability through surveillance. Risk management will identify actual and potential causes of patient accidents and will implement programs to eliminate or reduce these occurrences.

DOCTRINE OF CORPORATE NEGLIGENCE

The Doctrine of Corporate Negligence means that the hospital/ medical center or healthcare agency as an entity is negligent. It is the failure of the corporation to follow an established standard of conduct to which all healthcare corporations should conform in a given situation. The doctrine of corporate negligence or liability is relatively new. The determination of negligence is based on violations or breach of duty owed to the patient by the hospital/medical center or health center.

SAMPLE CASE: *DARLING* V. *CHARLESTON COMMUNITY HOSPITAL*

In the famous landmark decision of *Darling* v. *Charleston Community Hospital* (211 N.E. Second 53 (Illinois), 1965), Darling, the plaintiff, was an 18-year-old college student who played on the football team. Darling was injured while playing football and was taken to the emergency room of Charleston Community Hospital. The doctor on emergency call on that particular day was a general practitioner. The physician took x-rays and diagnosed fractures of both bones below the knee in the right leg. The doctor reduced the fractures and applied a cast to the leg.

Darling complained of pain continuously. Three days after applying the cast, the general practitioner split the cast. Darling continued to complain of pain. There was evidence that circulation was impaired, and there was a foul odor at the area of the fracture. There were no orthopedic specialists consulted at any time. Approximately two weeks later, Darling was transferred to another hospital and given the care of an orthopedic doctor, but it was too late. The leg was amputated.

The most important issue decided in the case was the standard of care for determining hospital liability. The court found the hospital failed to meet the standard of care due to Darling because neither a consultation for examination by a skilled orthopedic surgeon was utilized, nor were there insufficiently trained nurses capable of recognizing the progressive gangrenous condition that resulted in the leg amputation. The court allowed the rules and regulations of the Illinois State Department of Health, the Hospital Licensing Act, and the standards of the Joint Commission on the Accreditation of Health Care Organizations to be introduced as evidence. The verdict against the hospital was $100,000. The physician settled prior to the trial for $40,000. The hospital was found liable under the Doctrine of Corporate Negligence. The court states, "The governing body of each hospital shall be responsible for the operation of the hospital, for the selection of medical staff, and for the quality of care.

Responsibility of Professional Staff

A physician is an independent contractor who alone is responsible for the exercise of professional skill and judgment. The staff physician is *not* subject to control by the hospital/medical center in the execution of his/her services, and the hospital/medical center assumes responsibility. The governing body of the hospital/medical center or healthcare center is the board of trustees. The board is charged with the right and the duty to monitor the quality of healthcare being provided by the professional staff. The board members must carefully scrutinize the reports submitted by the professional staff and must assure themselves that there is continuous review, analysis, and evaluation of patient care.

SAMPLE CASE: *GONZALES V. NORK*

In California in 1974, Dr. Nork, an orthopedist, was found negligent in his care of at least 30 patients (*Gonzales* v. *Nork,* California Supreme Court, November 19, 1973). The verdict was $3,710,447, of which $2,000,000 constituted *punitive damages* because of Dr. Nork's wanton, reckless disregard of the patients in his care.

The evidence in the case showed that the hospital, the medical staff, and the staff licensing board never took any action against Dr. Nork although it knew, or "should have known," he was causing injury to his patients.

The suit was brought by Albert Gonzales. The facts briefly were that Mr. Gonzales was examined by Dr. Nork in November 1967, for back pain. Dr. Nork diagnosed a herniated disc. A lumbar myelogram was done and was interpreted as normal. In spite of this and without consultation, Dr. Nork performed a laminectomy and spinal fusion on Mr. Gonzales. Albert Gonzales complained of pain immediately after surgery in his back, legs, and right thigh. There were conflicting reports on Mr. Gonzales' medical records. A November 30 report by Dr. Nork stated, "Patient had done extremely well, no complaints" (Hemelt & Mackert, 1982, p. 33). The nurses' notes of the same date stated, "Ambulated with help for ten minutes, had to be helped to the bathroom, complains of pain continuously, left leg felt paralyzed" (Hemelt & Mackert, 1982, p. 33). Mr. Gonzales became progressively worse; three years later Mr. Gonzales became permanently disabled.

Mercy Hospital, where Mr. Gonzales was a patient, was also found liable for negligence under the Doctrine of Corporate Negligence. The court held that the hospital owed the patient a duty of care that included protecting the patient from acts of medical negligence by the hospital's staff physicians. The words used were, "If the hospital knows, or has reason to know, or should have known such acts were likely to occur" (Hemelt & Mackert, 1982, p. 34). The court held that the hospital was corporately responsible for the conduct of the medical staff. The courts expect hospitals to have policies and procedures to reasonably assure proper patient care and to take appropriate action against those who do not comply.

DOCTOR-OWNED HOSPITAL/CLINIC LIABILITY

There has been a recent surge of clinics and emergency care centers in operation. Under California state statutes, operation of a clinic owned by a physician will make the physician liable not only for his/her own acts, but also for the conduct of his/her employees (i.e., nurses, radiologic technologists). The law is very explicit about paramedical personnel performing various acts above the legal jurisdiction. A radiologic technologist is not licensed to draw blood unless the individual has the appropriate phlebotomist certification on file with the State Department of Health Services. Ordering nurses and/or medical assistants to perform radiographic procedures without the appropriate state licensure is not legal. Many radiographers working in doctor-owned clinics and/or offices have indicated that as long as the physician gives his/her permission to perform duties that are beyond the scope and practice, it is permissible. *NOT SO!* Any duty out of the scope and practice of licensure is *illegal.* No job is worth doing something that could be a detriment to the patient, or making an individual an accessory to a criminal act. It is imperative to make sure that you know the extent of malpractice for yourself when employed in a physician's clinic/office. Most doctors may not have malpractice for their employees due to the high insurance premiums. It would be advisable to have your own personal malpractice insurance, which can be purchased through the American Society of Radiologic Technologists.

GOOD SAMARITAN LAWS

The main purpose of the Good Samaritan Laws was to encourage citizens to assist their fellow man by rendering emergency medical aid to injured persons. These laws were passed to protect the same citizens from civil or criminal liability for any acts or omissions resulting from attempts to give such emergency medical aid. These laws vary in their particular coverage from state to state. Some states limit coverage to healthcare professionals, while other states cover every citizen who gives emergency aid.

In spite of rumors or statements to the contrary, there are no reported cases of successful lawsuits against any physicians stopping to give emergency aid. There is still concern among healthcare professionals (i.e., radiographers) regarding potential liability in emergency situations. But it is evident from the legislation passed that state legislators, in general, regard persons who give emergency care as a protected class. The individual who in good faith renders emergency care at the scene of an accident shall not be liable for any civil damages as a result of any acts or omissions in rendering emergency care. The first Good Samaritan Law was passed in California in 1959. Since that time, other states have followed California's lead to include various categories of healthcare professionals, including radiographers.

DUTY OF CARE

Anyone may render aid in an emergency situation, but under English and American law, no one is forced to do so where there is no duty. If there is no relationship between parties involved, then no duty arises. On the other hand, if one elects to render assistance in an emergency, then one must meet certain standards of skill and competency. The essential element or test of malpractice is the "reasonable man test." What would a reasonable, prudent radiographer do in the particular circumstance? If the radiographer responded appropriately as a reasonable person and the standard of care has been met, there would be no negligence. It is the act of giving aid that creates a relationship between the victim and the good samaritan, and consequently, a duty arises to render due care.

It is also necessary to understand that the statutes do not immunize one from being sued. But if, and when, a person is sued, the defense of the Good Samaritan immunity would be raised to show that the individual being sued qualifies under the state Good Samaritan statute and is entitled to immunity (Hemelt & Mackert, 1982, p. 51).

HOSPITAL LIABILITY AND MALPRACTICE

Hospital liability and malpractice insurance, also known as "patient liability insurance," is intended to cover all claims against the hospital arising out of alleged negligence of any member of the physician staff and/or employees. The usual kinds of insurance carried by a hospital are:

1. Public liability.

2. Products and druggists' liability.

3. Elevator liability.

4. Worker's compensation.

5. Steam boiler insurance.

6. Sprinkler leakage.

7. Safe burglary protection.

8. Hospital liability.

9. Automobile personal injury.

10. Fidelity and surety bonds.

11. Fire insurance.

12. Electrical machinery.

13. Radium hazards.

One hospital may have ten different malpractice attorneys in adjusting claims and incidents that may occur on a daily basis.

Injury Reporting and Recording

Hospital employees are instructed to report any injury to a patient to the administration via the department manager and/or nursing supervisor, who, in turn, should report it immediately to the insurance carrier. Failure to give notice to the insurance carrier, in the case of an injury, may be a good reason to disclaim the policy and may make it easier to award damages to the injured party in a legal case. Even when the hospital makes an investigation and, in good faith, relying on the investigation, concludes that there is no liability or that the accident was too trivial to report and makes no report, the hospital then acts at its own risk. The insurance carrier may cancel the policy, and the hospital then is responsible for legal counsel and damages.

A patient was lying on the x-ray table and had her left hand underneath the table. She did not speak English, so communication was a bit difficult. The student technologist pushed the fluoroscopic tower up and out of the way, and the patient's middle finger was crushed under the roller wheels of the fluoroscopic tower. There was no visible injury, and she never mentioned that she was injured. The patient left the radiology department without mentioning the injury to anyone. One week later, the radiology manager received a letter from the patient's attorney with a copy of a letter from the orthopedic surgeon who had treated her broken finger. A negligence action suit was filed against the hospital, the student technologist, and the x-ray manufacturing company. Since there was no mention of an injury or incident report from the hospital, the doctrine of res ipsa loquitur applied in this case. The hospital paid damages of $3,750.18 to the patient. *Make sure that you check the condition of the patient at all times, even at discharge.*

SAMPLE CASE: NEGLIGENCE FOUND IN X-RAY PATIENT'S FALL FROM TABLE

A university was obligated to indemnify a medical clinic for the negligence of a university employee working at the clinic, a Hawaii appellate court ruled. A patient was admitted to the clinic for a barium enema. A university student, acting under the general supervision of the clinic's employees, attached the standard footrest to the x-ray table and placed the patient on the table. When a physician employed by the clinic tilted the x-ray table, the footrest detached, and the patient fell. He was severely injured. The clinic agreed to settle the patient's claim against it for $150,690.08.

The clinic then sued the university for indemnity under an agreement between them. Under the agreement, students in a radiology technology program at the university obtain clinical experience at the clinic. The university agreed to indemnify the clinic from claims and expenses for negligent acts of its employees and students. A jury found the clinic 70 percent responsible for the patient's injuries.

On appeal, the decision was affirmed. The university was ordered to pay the clinic 30 percent of the settlement amount and the clinic's $57,913.01 costs and fees. The court stated the indemnity was not limited to damages caused solely by a student or employee of the university (*Straub Clinic and Hospital* v. *Chicago Insurance Company*, 665 P. Second 176, Hawaii Intermediate Court of Appeals, June 8, 1983).

VIGNETTE 11—POOR PATIENT CARE
CAUSES BACK INJURY

Frank Filter, a patient at Coulomb Memorial Medical Center, was scheduled for abdominal surgery. In a weak and frail state due to a long-term illness, Frank Filter needed a special radiographic examination. When Frank Filter arrived in the radiology department, he questioned the radiographer, Amy Afterglow, R.T., about the pending procedure. Amy Afterglow had told him, rather abruptly, that his doctor had ordered the study and that if he had any questions, Mr. Filter should ask his doctor. In a curt manner, Amy Afterglow questioned Mr. Filter as to whether or not he wanted the study completed, since there was no time to waste. Mr. Filter agreed to the procedure.

Mr. Filter was quickly and roughly pulled onto a cold, hard x-ray table. The jerky movement hurt his back. During the procedure, he was very uncomfortable due to the severe back pain.

Mr. Filter had asked for a cushion to be placed under his buttocks to ease the pain. Amy Afterglow had told him to just hold still and cooperate or else he would be sent back to his room and the procedure would be cancelled. Mr. Filter cooperated.

When the radiographic procedure was completed, Mr. Filter was once again pulled roughly onto the stretcher. Again he experienced severe back pain. He was rolled onto a cold, drafty hallway to await patient transport.

Time passed, and Mr. Filter's back pain became more severe. He was experiencing numbness and tingling in his right foot and leg. Other staff radiographers passed him in the hallway and ignored his complaint of lower back pain.

When the patient transporter finally arrived, Mr. Filter was in tears due to the severe pain. When Mr. Filter reached his bed, he told the nurse, Greta Grid, R.N., that he had severe back pain from being pulled onto the x-ray table. Greta Grid was quiet huffy and made it clear that the pain was due to lying on the hard table and not from being pulled or pushed onto it.

That evening, Mr. Filter told his physician that he had received a back injury when he was pulled onto the x-ray table. Mr. Filter's physician ordered a lumbar spine series that evening, and Mr. Filter was diagnosed as having a subluxation of the fifth lumbar vertebrae.

Who would be liable for Mr. Filter's injuries? What, if any, legal implications or legal risks are involved?

ANSWER

Since Mr. Filter did not have an existing back problem upon admittance to Coulomb Memorial Medical Center, there is a legal risk for Amy Afterglow, Greta Grid, and the medical center. Everyone working in Coulomb Memorial Medical Center has the obligation to provide proper care to patients. This includes protecting the patient from any harm or injury. Meeting the standard of care due a patient protects Coulomb Memorial Medical Center. Amy Afterglow was careless in her rough handling of Mr. Filter. She should have asked other staff to assist her in moving Mr. Filter onto the x-ray table. Greta Grid was negligent in not reporting Mr. Filter's back complaint to his physician and documenting the occurrence of his injury by the radiographer. Coulomb Memorial Medical Center should be held liable, under the Doctrine of Corporate Negligence, for Mr. Filter's back injury received by its employees.

VIGNETTE 12—IMPROPER COMMUNICATION SITUATION

Mrs. Bremsstrahlung, who spoke and understood very little English, was an outpatient at Compton Clinic. Mrs. Bremsstrahlung was scheduled for radiographs of both feet. After a brief introduction, the radiographer, Paul Penumbra, R.T., directed the patient to the x-ray suite. Paul Penumbra told Mrs. Bremsstrahlung to remove both shoes and get up on the table.

Paul Penumbra immediately left the room to get the proper detailed cassettes for the procedure. A few minutes later, Paul Penumbra arrived in the x-ray suite to find Mrs. Bremsstrahlung standing on top of the x-ray table. Paul Penumbra began to laugh and told Mrs. Bremsstrahlung that he did not want her to stand on the table, but instead to lay on her back. In a frenzy of embarrassment, Mrs. Bremsstrahlung hit her head on the x-ray tube housing, causing a laceration across her forehead.

What, if any, legal implications or legal risks are involved?

ANSWER

Patients are very cooperative and responsive to questions and directions, given they understand what is being asked or stated. Therefore, reinforcing the importance of clear and accurate communication between patients and radiographers is necessary. Patients will do exactly what we ask them to do. However, by monitoring a patient more closely, a radiographer will reduce injuries resulting from miscommunication.

Paul Penumbra should have stayed in the x-ray suite to assist Mrs. Bremsstrahlung onto the x-ray table. More importantly, Paul Penumbra was careless in not making certain that Mrs. Bremsstrahlung understood the instructions. Paul Penumbra and Compton Clinic should be held liable for Mrs. Bremsstrahlung's injuries.

ENDNOTE

1. Facing the risk. *R.T. Image*, August 10, 1992.

REVIEW QUESTIONS

1. Regarding the Doctrine of Corporate Negligence, the *Darling* v. *Charleston Community Hospital* case found the hospital failed to meet the standard of _____ due to Darling.

    a.   Reasonableness.

    b.   Injury.

    c.   Care.

    d.   Duty.

2. The medical staff physicians are subjected to the control of the _____ in the execution of their services.

    a.   Hospital administrator.

    b.   Medical staff secretary.

    c.   Governing body.

    d.   None of the above.

3. In the *Gonzales* v. *Nork* case, the court held that the hospital was _____ for the conduct of the medical staff.

    a.   Not liable.

    b.   Corporately responsible.

    c.   Negligent.

    d.   None of the above.

4. Any duty out of the scope and practice of state licensure would be considered:

    a.   Lawful.

    b.   Careless.

    c.   Negligent.

    d.   Illegal.

5. Reporting of patient injuries is documented in the:

    a.   Patient progress notes form.

    b.   Physician's notes form.

    c.   Nursing notes form.

    d.   Incident report form.

CHAPTER SIX

DOCTRINE OF INFORMED CONSENT

Upon completion of Chapter 6, the reader will be able to:

1. Define the Doctrine of Informed Consent.

2. Discuss the preparation of an informed consent.

3. Assess the verification of an informed consent.

4. Recognize the legality of an informed consent.

5. Discuss the concepts of (a) who may sign a consent, (b) spouses' consent, and (c) rescinding a consent.

6. Differentiate radiologic procedures that are involved in informed-consent lawsuits.

THE PATIENT'S RIGHT TO KNOW

This doctrine could more appropriately be called "the patient's right to know and participate in his own healthcare." Informed consent is a doctrine that has evolved sociologically with the changing times. The courts have mandated that every patient is entitled to an informed consent before any procedure can be performed. Judge Benjamin Cordozo, while serving on the court of appeals of New York in a 1914 case, established that every adult has the right to determine what is to be done to his body (*Schloendorf* v. *Soc. of New York Hosp.*, 211 N.Y. 125, 105 N.E. 92, 1914). Judge Cordozo indicated that a surgeon who performs an operation without the patient's consent may be liable for assault and battery. An assault is the threat to do bodily harm to an individual. The act of doing the physical harm is the battery. It is, therefore, necessary for patients to consent to surgery or medical procedures in order for a charge of assault and battery to be avoided. Consent is the affirmation by the patient to have his/her body touched by certain designated individuals such as the doctor, nurse, radiographer, and others.

In *Cobb* v. *Grant*, supra, the California Supreme Court held that a patient must be given the opportunity to provide an "informed consent" prior to the performance of certain medical procedures and treatment. The court stated that in order to give an "informed consent," the patient had to be informed of

1. the nature of the treatment;

2. any risk, complications, and expected benefits or effects of such treatment; and

3. any alternatives to the procedure and their risks and benefits.

The patient's informed consent, as distinguished from consent, is not required for all medical procedures and treatment. In identifying circumstances where an informed consent is required, the court distinguished between those procedures that it labeled "complex" and those that it labeled "simple" and "common."

RADIOLOGIC PROCEDURES INVOLVED IN INFORMED-CONSENT LAWSUITS

Excretory urography was the radiologic procedure most commonly involved in informed-consent litigation. In comparison with angiographic and myelographic procedures, the relative risk of serious injuries from excretory urography is so low that even though the total number of excretory urograms is greater than that for the other procedures, fewer injuries might be expected. The lower the frequency of risk disclosure to patients for urography compared with angiography and myelography may well explain why it is involved in a greater number of informed-consent lawsuits.

Spring et al. (1988) have reported that informed-consent lawsuits involved excretory urography about six times as often as contrast material-enhanced computed tomography (CT). The two procedures have the same number of lawsuits pending. The study suggests that an increase in the number of newer contrast studies (e.g., CT or digital subtraction angiography) may result in an increase in informed-consent lawsuits.

Informed consent was considered by the defendant radiologist to be a significant factor in most of the reported lawsuits involving angiographic procedures. In ten (91 percent) of eleven lawsuits, the defendant radiologist made an effort to obtain an informed consent that was documented. All but one of these lawsuits resulted in favorable outcomes for the defense. Angiography is ordinarily perceived as having a higher risk of injury than other radiological procedures and, therefore, more frequently involves a documented effort to obtain informed consent. This may explain the lower incidence of lawsuits instigated and favorable outcomes for the plaintiff (Spring et al., 1988, p. 248).

PREPARATION OF AN INFORMED CONSENT

A physician who prepares an informed consent should prepare the form by setting forth medical information with respect to the nature of the procedure or treatment, its expected benefits or effects, its possible risks and complications, and the alternatives to the proposed treatment or procedure and their possible risks and complications. The form must be supplemented either through verbal discussions with the patient and/or through written additions that set forth such information. These forms are helpful only if they can be understood by the patient. Therefore, it is extremely important for the medical information set forth in such forms to be written in clear, simple, and easily understood terms. In addition, it is absolutely essential for such forms to clearly state that the patient should ask any and all questions he/she may have about the proposed procedure. A copy of the informed consent should be placed in the patient's medical records.

VERIFICATION OF INFORMED CONSENT

The physician (radiologist), not the hospital, has the fiduciary duty to disclose all information relevant to the patient's decision and to obtain the patient's informed consent. Further, obtaining informed consent involves the practice of medicine, in which the hospital and its employees should not intervene. Hospital employees are not licensed or qualified to adequately explain the various types of medical procedures to the patient and to respond to the patient's potential questions. Only the physician has both the technical knowledge and the background knowledge of the particular patient's condition necessary to assure that an adequate disclosure of information, including that pertaining to the risks of treatment, has been given for *that patient* and that proper responses have been given to the patient's questions.

Hospital personnel (radiographers) cannot and should not be responsible for securing the patient's informed consent (and concomitantly, giving the patient the information that is required in order to secure the patient's informed consent); it can be expected that patients will ask hospital staff who are performing a procedure pursuant to the doctor's (radiologist's) orders questions about what they will be or are doing. Radiographers generally may answer such questions; however, if it appears that the patient has significant questions about the nature of the procedure and its benefits or risks that indicate he/she may not have been given sufficient information about the procedure or understood the information he/she was given, the radiographer should contact the patient's physician and/or radiologist in order to allow him/her to answer the questions and thereby help to assure that the patient has given an informed consent to the procedure.

It must be understood that the radiographer is not the one performing the fluoroscopic procedure the patient is about to undergo. The radiographer does not have the necessary information, nor does he/she know what alternative radiographic procedures are available for the patient. Radiographers should not allow themselves to be placed in the ridiculous position of "witnessing the patient's signature." It is common practice for the radiographer to have the function of getting the patient to sign the radiological procedure consent form. The radiographer, generally, may not be present when the patient's physician or radiologist presumably gave the necessary instructions and explanations to the patient. The radiographer could be held personally liable if he/she knew, or should have known, the patient was uninformed and did not take remedial measures. The hospital could also be held liable under the doctrine of corporate negligence or respondeat superior if, through its personnel, the hospital knew, or had reason to know, that physicians (radiologists) or staff personnel are performing procedures without a bona fide consent. The radiographer has a professional obligation to protect his/her employer's interests. Since the hospital has an obligation to see that the patient is informed, the radiographer would be decreasing the legal risk to the hospital by informing the physician (radiologist) of the patient's needs.

LEGALITY OF INFORMED CONSENTS

It is basic that the intentional touching of another without his/her consent could be construed as a legal wrong constituting assault, battery, or both. *Consent* is the affirmation by the patient to have his/her body touched by certain designated individuals such as a doctor, nurse, radiographer, or others. There are different classifications of consents. There is *implied consent*. When a patient rolls up his/her sleeve to receive an injection, this action can be construed as giving consent to the procedure. An *expressed consent*, as the term implies, is an affirmative action or statement to signify one's intention. There are also verbal and written consents. An oral or verbal consent is binding. The problem arises when it comes to a question of *evidentiary matter*. It might be difficult to prove the patient gave an oral consent. Even where witnesses are present and hear the consent given, their testimony might not be consistent on details and could weaken their credibility. A written consent obviously offers some tangible proof that the patient voluntarily signed a form. It is subject to scrutiny and disbelief if other facts relevant to the situation indicate that the patient did not fully and intelligently understand what the affixing of his/her signature meant in relation to his/her medical care.

A proper consent form is an important evidentiary document in the event of a dispute regarding the claim that an informed consent was not given. The signed consent would generally be considered presumptive evidence that information about a particular act was given. The individual giving consent must be mentally competent and able to appreciate the material facts. The patient must have consented voluntarily, based on sufficient knowledge and information to make an intelligent decision.

RESCINDING CONSENT

The patient may rescind the consent given either verbally or in writing at any time. A written consent may be rescinded verbally. Any time a patient withdraws his/her consent, it is as though he/she had never given a consent. This means that any procedure done on a patient who has rescinded his/her consent would be a battery.

WHO MAY CONSENT

The patient upon whom the procedure is to be performed is the only one who has authority over his/her body as long as he/she is conscious and competent. The consent is invalid if the patient is intoxicated, under the influence of narcotics, delirious, and/or irrational. It is essential to respect the individual's right to make his/her own decisions. If the patient is mentally incompetent, consent must be obtained from a person legally authorized to give consent for the patient. For example, an elderly or infirm person may have had the foresight to authorize a power of attorney designating a child or relative to act in his/her behalf.

Spouse's Consent

Can a husband consent to his wife's operation or radiology procedure in a nonemergency situation? The answer is clearly *no*. And the converse is true. The wife has no authority to consent for the husband.

Minor's Consent

A minor is considered to be under the jurisdiction of his/her parents until the age of majority. In most states, including California, the age of majority is 18 years. The minor may consent for his/her own care if married, emancipated, pregnant, suffering from venereal disease, or in need of psychological or psychiatric care. The term "emancipated" means the individual is no longer under the control of another. Generally, this occurs where a minor is working and is responsible for his/her own support and necessities.

The common law holds that the natural parents or legal guardians of a child have the authority to consent to medical care for the minor. The parent is presumed to act in the best interest of the child, and therefore, there is a presumption that the child will be protected. There are times when parents, because of religious beliefs, will not permit the child to receive medical care that society believes is in the best interest of the child. In these circumstances, the state must exercise its right under the parens patriae doctrine and intervene to protect the health of the child. The law may not interfere with religious convictions, but it may interfere with religious practice. Religious belief is not a lawful excuse for breach of duty to provide medical care for a child. The rights of religion and parenthood are not beyond the limitations of the Fourteenth Amendment of the U.S. Constitution.

California statute permits medical treatment without parental consent to children for illness and injury during regular school hours unless there is written objection from the parents.

SAMPLE CASE: PATIENT CAN SUE FOR FAILURE TO OBTAIN HER INFORMED CONSENT

A patient's voluntary dismissal of a claim of negligent treatment did not result in dismissal of her claim for failure to obtain informed consent, a North Carolina appellate court ruled. The patient brought an action against radiologists alleging that they failed to adequately inform her of the known hazards of radiation therapy and therefore did not obtain her informed consent for treatment. She also alleged negligence in administering the radiation. The treatment resulted in severe radiation damage to her intestines.

The patient voluntarily dismissed her claim based on negligence in rendering medical services. The radiologists alleged that her claim of lack of informed consent was barred by the statute of limitations. The trial court granted their motion to dismiss.

On appeal, the radiologists contended that the patient took a voluntary dismissal on the question of their failure to obtain informed consent, arguing that "rendering medical services" included obtaining the informed consent to the treatment as well as the actual treatment. The court found that the word "*rendering*" applied to performance of the medical procedure and that the informed-consent claim was not voluntarily dismissed.

The radiologists also contended that uninformed or invalid consent was the same as no consent at all, and therefore, the subsequent treatment constituted unauthorized touching or battery. Thus, the action would be controlled by the one-year statute of limitations for battery.

The court found that the claim was for malpractice based on failure to disclose the various choices with regard to the proposed treatment and the dangers involved, and that the three-year statute of limitations applied. Holding the patient's claim was not barred, the court reversed the trial court's judgment (*Nelson* v. *Patrick*, 293 S.E. Second 829 North Carolina Court of Appeals, August 3, 1982, *The Citation*, 46(8), pp. 89–90).

VIGNETTE 13—INFORMED CONSENT

Mrs. Ula Umbra is a 60-year-old female admitted to Resolution Hospital for a coronary angiogram. Mrs. Umbra has signed the routine consent form as required by the hospital. This was done in admitting and witnessed by the admission clerk.

During the course of preparing Mrs. Umbra for the coronary angiogram, Gerry Generator, R.T., talks to Mrs. Umbra about healthcare in general. Mrs. Umbra states to Gerry Generator, R.T., "My doctor has not discussed this procedure with me, but I guess he will before it begins, won't he?" Gerry Generator asks Mrs. Umbra if she read and signed the consent form. Mrs. Umbra states, "I read the consent form, but I really don't understand what is going to be done."

What, if any, obligation does Gerry Generator, R.T., have toward Mrs. Ula Umbra? Would Gerry Generator, R.T., be liable if Mrs. Umbra had the coronary angiogram under the above circumstances?

ANSWER

Gerry Generator, R.T., has several obligations. There is an obligation to the patient, the physician, and Resolution Hospital. When it becomes evident that the patient, Mrs. Umbra, has either not been fully informed of the coronary angiogram or does not understand the implications of the procedure, the patient's physician performing the procedure should be notified immediately.

The radiographer should document the situation and the fact that the physician was notified. The radiographer has an obligation to inform the patient's physician of the patient's statement so that corrective measures may be taken by the doctor.

Resolution Hospital has no direct obligation to inform the patient of the coronary angiogram to be done. In fact, it cannot do so since only the physician knows what techniques and specific procedures will be utilized for the specific patient. However, Resolution Hospital could be held as a party-defendant by the patient alleging no consent was given; therefore, the radiographer should take all reasonable measures to protect the hospital.

The radiographer should also protect himself, because the patient could include the radiographer as a party-defendant. The patient has put the radiographer on notice that she is uninformed regarding her imminent coronary angiogram. The radiographer should notify the physician, the supervising radiographer, and any other appropriate parties of the situation. Otherwise, the radiographer could be held liable if the coronary angiogram were performed without the patient's consent.

VIGNETTE 14—INFORMED CONSENT SITUATION

Vicky Volt, R.T., is a staff radiographer at Incandescent General Hospital. Ms. Molly Milliampere is scheduled for a lumbar myelogram. Vicky Volt, R.T., is responsible for obtaining a consent signed by Ms. Milliampere consenting to the lumbar myelogram. As Vicky Volt, R.T., begins to explain the procedure to Ms. Milliampere, the patient asks that her daughter be contacted to give permission before the procedure begins. Vicky Volt, R.T., has tried several times to contact Ms. Milliampere's daughter but is unable to reach her. The radiologist, Doctor Ohm, states that he has to go ahead with the procedure because the patient is scheduled for surgery immediately after the lumbar myelogram.

What, if anything, should Vicky Volt do? Can Doctor Ohm proceed with the lumbar myelogram? If so, under what circumstances? What, if any, legal liabilities could be involved?

ANSWER

There is nothing in the situation to indicate that Ms. Milliampere is not competent and capable of consenting to the procedure herself. The patient may consent or withhold consent for medical treatment or procedure. The fact that Ms. Milliampere wants her daughter contacted should be respected. The daughter should be notified as requested. Ms. Milliampere may wish to consult with her daughter before submitting to the lumbar myelogram. However, the daughter's consent cannot be substituted for Ms. Milliampere's consent. The fact that Ms. Milliampere is 72 years old has no bearing on her right to make decisions regarding her own body. Unless there is some evidence of incompetency or inability, only Ms. Milliampere can give an informed consent for the procedure.

Doctor Ohm could proceed with the lumbar myelogram only if Ms. Milliampere gave an informed consent. It would be wise and good business for the daughter to be incorporated into the consent procedure since the patient specifically requested this, but the daughter cannot authorize the procedure where the patient is capable of consenting. It is not an emergency at this point, and Dr. Ohm could not proceed under the Emergency Rule. He must have the patient's valid consent.

If the preceding was not done in accord with general practice in procuring consents and the patient could establish she did not give a valid consent, the physician, radiographer, and hospital might be sued and found liable for assault and battery.

POSTSCRIPT TO VIGNETTES 13 AND 14

The First Amendment guarantees the integrity of one's body. Any touching of an individual's body without appropriate authority or the individual's consent could be construed as an assault and battery. The courts recognize assault and battery as giving rise to a criminal action for which the law gives a remedy in money damages.

The hospital and its employees, as well as the doctors, can be held liable for performing treatment or procedures without the patient's consent. The courts apply the doctrine of corporate liability, respondeat superior, or other appropriate law and, where it can be ascertained that the hospital, as in this case, knew or should have known there was no bona fide informed consent by the patient and did not correct the situation but permitted uninformed procedures, the radiographer, physician, and hospital are at legal risk.

Some criteria should be met by the radiographer to assure that proper consent is obtained. The patient must be conscious and able to comprehend the document that is being signed. There should be a reasonable belief on the part of the radiographer that the patient has been informed regarding the nature and purpose of the procedure and the possible risks related to it. The patient should be able to read, write, and understand the language being used for communication. The patient should be consenting to the procedure freely, voluntarily, and without any coercion—"of his own will."

REVIEW QUESTIONS

1. The California State Supreme Court indicated that in an informed consent, the patient must be informed of the following except:

    a.   Nature of the treatment.

    b.   Reasonable response to requests.

    c.   Risks, complications, and benefits.

    d.   Alternatives to the procedures.

2. The _____ has the fiduciary duty to obtain the patient's informed consent.

    a.   Radiographer.

    b.   Physician.

    c.   Hospital.

    d.   Nurse.

3. A written consent may be rescinded verbally or in writing at any time.

    a.   True.

    b.   False.

4. A consent is invalid under the following patient conditions except:

    a.   Intoxication.

    b.   Sanity.

    c.   Delirium.

    d.   Drugged.

5. A minor may consent for care if the following conditions exist:

    a.   Emancipated.

    b.   Pregnant.

    c.   In need of psychological care.

    d.   All of the above.

6. California law permits medical treatment without parental consent during:

    a.   A sport event.

    b.   School hours.

    c.   Babysitting hours.

    d.   None of the above.

CHAPTER SEVEN

ETHICS

Upon completion of Chapter 7, the reader will be able to:

1. Differentiate between morals, ethics, and law.

2. Describe the Code of Ethics of the American Registry of Radiologic Technologists.

3. Define euthanasia.

4. Recognize the responsibilities and accountability for humanistic behavior in providing healthcare to the patient.

Unlike legal issues where a statute or judicial decision can be referred to for guidance, the ethical area is subject to philosophical, theological, and individual interpretation of what is right or wrong in a particular situation.

THE DISTINCTION BETWEEN MORALS, ETHICS, AND LAW

Morality is fundamentally the inner conscience. Morality is one's concept of what is right or wrong as it relates to that conscience, to God,

95

a higher being, or to one's atheistic logical rationalization. Morality could be defined as fidelity to conscience.

Ethics is the principle of morality, including both the science of the good and the nature of the right, or the rules of conduct recognized with respect to a particular class of human actions. A broader conceptual definition is that ethics is primarily concerned with the good of the individual, concentrating on motives and attitudes. Ethical sanctions are internal and appeal to one's honor, conscience, or what is good for society. Every profession, including radiography, has a code of ethics which serves as a guide for professional conduct.

Legal concepts are distinguishable from ethics. *Law* is defined as the sum total of man-made rules and regulations by which society is governed in a formal and legally binding manner. The law mandates certain acts and forbids certain other acts under penalty of criminal sanction, such as a fine or imprisonment, or of civil action. The law is primarily concerned with society's good as a functioning unit, while the primary concern of ethics is with the good of the individual within the society. Therefore, a radiographer or a healthcare professional who would take the life of a terminally ill patient, no matter how noble the motivation, would be subject to a charge of murder.

CODE OF ETHICS OF THE AMERICAN REGISTRY OF RADIOLOGIC TECHNOLOGISTS

This code of ethics is to serve as a guide by which radiologic technologists may evaluate their professional conduct as it relates to patients, colleagues, other members of the allied professions and healthcare consumers. The code of ethics is not law, but is intended to assist radiologic technologists in maintaining a high level of ethical conduct and in providing for the protection, safety, and comfort of patients.

Principle 1

The Radiologic Technologist conducts him/herself in a professional manner, responds to patient needs, and supports colleagues and associates in providing quality patient care.

Principle 2

The Radiologic Technologist acts to advance the principle objective of the profession to provide services to humanity with full respect for the dignity of mankind.

Principle 3

The Radiologic Technologist delivers patient care and services unrestricted by the concerns of personal attributes or the nature of the disease or illness, and without discrimination regardless of sex, race, creed, religion, or socioeconomic status.

Principle 4

The Radiologic Technologist practices technology founded upon theoretical knowledge and concepts, utilizes equipment and accessories consistent with the purposes for which they have been designed, and employs procedures and techniques appropriately.

Principle 5

The Radiologic Technologist assesses situations, exercises care, discretion and judgement, assumes responsibility for professional decisions, and acts in the best interest of the patient.

Principle 6

The Radiologic Technologist acts as an agent through observation and communication to obtain pertinent information for the physician to aid in the diagnosis and treatment management of the patient, and recognizes that interpretation and diagnosis are outside the scope and practice for the profession.

Principle 7

The Radiologic Technologist uses equipment and accessories, employs techniques and procedures, performs services in accordance with an accepted standard of practice, and demonstrates expertise in minimizing the radiation exposure to the patient, self, and other members of the healthcare team.

Principle 8

The Radiologic Technologist practices ethical conduct appropriate to the profession, and protects the patient's right to quality radiologic technology care.

Principle 9

The Radiologic Technologist respects confidences entrusted in the course of professional practice, respects the patient's right to privacy, and reveals confidential information only as required by law or to protect the welfare of the individual or the community.

Principle 10

The Radiologic Technologist continually strives to improve knowledge and skills by participating in educational and professional activities, sharing knowledge with colleagues, and investigating new and innovative aspects of professional practice. One means available to improve knowledge and skill is through professional continuing education.

RULES OF ETHICS FROM THE AMERICAN REGISTRY OF RADIOLOGIC TECHNOLOGISTS

The Rules of Ethics form the second part of the Standards of Ethics. They are mandatory and directive-specific standards of minimally acceptable professional conduct for all present Registered Technologists and applicants. Certification is a method of assuring the medical community and the public that an individual is qualified to practice within the profession. Since the public relies on certificates and registrations issued by the ARRT, it is essential that Registered Technologists and applicants act consistently within these Rules of Ethics. These Rules are intended to promote the protection, safety, and comfort of patients. The Rules of Ethics are enforceable. Registered Technologists and applicants engaging in any of the following conduct or activities with respect to them have violated the Rules of Ethics and are subject to sanctions as described herein:

1. Employing fraud or deceit in procuring or attempting to procure, maintain, renew, or obtain reinstatement of (a) employment in radiologic technology or a state permit, license, or registration certificate to practice radiologic technology, such as by altering in any respect a certificate of registration with the ARRT; or (b) a certificate of registration with the ARRT.

2. Subverting or attempting to subvert ARRT's examination process. Conduct that subverts or attempts to subvert ARRT's examination process includes, but is not limited to

   a. Conduct that violates the security of ARRT examination materials, such as removing examination materials from an examination room, or having unauthorized possession of any portion of or information concerning a future, current, or previously administered examination of the ARRT, or disclosing information concerning any portion of a future, current, or previously administered examination of the ARRT, or disclosing what purports to be, or under all circumstances is likely to be understood by the recipient, as any portion of or "inside" information concerning any portion of a future, current, or previously administered examination of the ARRT.

   b. Conduct that in any way compromises ordinary standards of test administration, such as communicating with another examinee during administration of the examination, copying another examinee's answers, permitting another examinee to copy one's answers, or possessing unauthorized materials.

   c. Impersonating an examinee or permitting an impersonator to take the examination on one's own behalf.

3. Conviction of a crime, including a felony, a gross misdemeanor, or a misdemeanor. Conviction as used in this provision includes a criminal proceeding where a finding or

verdict of guilt is made or returned where the adjudication of guilt is either withheld or not entered, or a criminal proceeding where the individual enters a plea of guilty or nolo contendere.

4. Failure to report to the ARRT that charges regarding the person's permit, license, or registration certificate to practice radiologic technology are pending or have been resolved adversely to the individual in any state, territory, or county, or that the individual has been refused a permit, license, or registration certificate to practice radiologic technology by another state, territory, or country.

5. Failure or inability to perform radiologic technology with reasonable skill and safety.

6. Engaging in unprofessional conduct, including, but not limited to

   a. A departure from or failure to conform to applicable federal, state, or local government rules regarding radiologic technology practice, or, if no such rule exists, to the minimal standards of acceptable and prevailing radiologic technology practice, or

   b. Any radiologic technology practice that may create unnecessary danger to a patient's life, health, or safety. Actual injury to a patient need not be established under this clause.

7. Delegating or accepting the delegation of a radiologic technology function or any other prescribed healthcare function when the delegation or acceptance could reasonably be expected to create an unnecessary danger to a patient's life, health, or safety. Actual injury to a patient need not be established under this clause.

8. Actual or potential inability to practice radiologic technology with reasonable skill and safety to patients by reason of illness, use of alcohol, drugs, chemicals, or any other material, or as a result of any mental or physical condition.

9. Adjudication as mentally incompetent, mentally ill, a chemically dependent person, or a person dangerous to the public by a court of competent jurisdiction.

10. Engaging in any unethical conduct, including, but not limited to, conduct likely to deceive, defraud, or harm the public, or demonstrating a willful or careless disregard for the health, welfare, or safety of a patient. Actual injury need not be established under this clause.

11. Engaging in conduct with a patient that is sexual or may reasonably be interpreted by the patient as sexual, or in any verbal behavior that is seductive or sexually demeaning to a patient, or engaging in sexual exploitation of a patient or former patient. This does not apply to preexisting consensual relationships.

12. Revealing a privileged communication from or relating to a patient, except when otherwise required or permitted by law.

13. Knowingly engaging or assisting any person to engage in or otherwise participating in abusive or fraudulent billing practices, including violations of federal Medicare and Medicaid laws or state medical assistance laws.

14. Improper management of patient records, including failure to maintain adequate patient records or to furnish a patient record of report required by law or making or causing or permitting anyone to make false, deceptive, or misleading entry in any patient record.

15. Knowingly aiding, assisting, advising, or allowing a person without a current and appropriate state permit, license, or registration certificate or a current certificate of registration with ARRT to engage in the practice of radiologic technology, in a jurisdiction which requires a person to have such a current and appropriate state permit, license, or registration certificate or a current and appropriate certificate of registration with ARRT in order to practice radiologic technology in such jurisdiction.

16. Violating a rule adopted by any state board with competent jurisdiction, an order of such board, or state or federal law relating to the practice of radiologic technology, or a state or federal narcotics or control substance law.

17. Knowingly providing false or misleading information that is directly related to the care of a patient.

18. Practicing outside the scope of practice authorized by the individual's current state permit, license, or registration certificate or the individual's current certificate of registration with the ARRT.

19. Making a false statement or knowingly providing false information to ARRT or failing to cooperate with any investigation of the ARRT or the Ethics Committee.

20. Engaging in false, fraudulent, deceptive, or misleading communications to any person regarding the individual's education, training, credentials, experience, or qualifications, or the status of the individual's state permit, license, or registration certificate in radiologic technology or certificate of registration with the ARRT.

EUTHANASIA

All hospitals must now have written policies and procedures describing how patient rights are protected at their institutions. Healthcare organizations must establish policies and procedures on euthanasia.

In establishing such policies, healthcare providers must take into consideration state and federal law, the opinion of the primary physician, and the patient's wishes as documented in the patient's medical record.

The *Patient Self-Determination Act* of 1992 requires hospitals and nursing homes to inform incoming patients of their rights concerning the use of life-sustaining treatment. Patients can then choose to develop instructions as to what to do in the event such treatment becomes necessary.

HUMANISTIC HEALTHCARE

The law permits abortion and euthanasia. This may be in direct conflict with the radiographer's morals or ethics. There are many other instances where the law and ethics are not necessarily compatible. There are times when the two disciplines are so interrelated they are indistinguishable. Although similar at times, the two disciplines are not the same and should not be equated by the radiographer. Changing social definitions of the quality of life must be considered and integrated with clinical care.

The early Greek physicians recognized that sick people often get well if nothing is done to the patient. Their advice is appropriate today in the Latin phrase *vix medicatrix naturae*, which means "to recognize the healing power of nature."

Humanistic healthcare that is ethical provides an overall understanding of the implications of healthcare. It helps to analyze the various issues involved in ethical decisions and to make humanistic ethical decisions based on appropriate data and information. Finally, it familiarizes the radiographer with his/her responsibilities and accountability for humanistic behavior in giving healthcare to his/her patients.

DIFFERENCES BETWEEN ETHICS AND LAW

ETHICS	LAW
Internal	External
Concerned with motive	Concerned with acts or conduct
Concerned with the interests of the individual and society	Concerned with the interests of society
Right—something to which one has a morally justified claim	Right—power or privilege inherent in person or enforceable in a court of law

It is impossible to give a right or wrong answer to the ethical vignettes that follow. Therefore, the "answer" to the vignette will be a reaction to the situation in which various sides will be identified and presented. Various questions will be raised, and the reader should look at those questions with an open mind. Perhaps the reader will become aware of aspects of the problem about which he/she was previously ignorant. The purpose of this approach is to stimulate the reader to think of the multifaceted relationship of such complex ethical healthcare problems. The final and ultimate right or wrong answers are the province of the reader.

The reader should raise questions that are not always adequately addressed by the ultimate decision makers. It is hoped the implications of those decisions will be understood in a more profound way.

VIGNETTE 15—INTOXICATED RADIOLOGIST

Rita Rad, R.T., was a staff radiographer at Spatial Medical Center. Doctor Andrew Angstrom was the resident radiologist for the morning. Rita Rad had noticed that Doctor Angstrom appeared to have been drinking when he arrived at the department. Doctor Angstrom was short tempered and a definite odor of alcohol was present on his breath.

Rita Rad was preparing Ms. Barbara Blooming for the scheduled intravenous pyelogram. Doctor Angstrom was called to inject the contrast media into Ms. Blooming. After the injection, Doctor Angstrom said, "I'm going over to the cafeteria for a cup of coffee." As soon as Doctor Angstrom left the x-ray suite, Ms. Blooming turned to Rita Rad and said, "He smells like a brewery. He's drunk, isn't he? Does he know what he's doing in that condition?"

What, if anything, is the appropriate response under these circumstances? What is the ethical issue involved? What is the radiographer's ethical duty and responsibility to the patient, to Spatial Hospital, and to the radiologist?

ANSWER

Value components exist in every medical decision. The radiologist has pledged loyalty to the profession, expressed in the traditional Hippocratic Oath and the American Medical Association Code of Ethics. Certain behavior is dictated by the professional organization.

The concern for the patient's competent care is not the issue. The question is, does the patient have a right to a truthful answer? Is the duty to tell the truth unconditional? Could it be argued that an intentional untruth is in the patient's best interest? Or is truth telling an independent act which is always required regardless of harmful consequences resulting from the truthful disclosure? The fundamental question—is it morally acceptable to withhold requested information that is potentially meaningful to a patient?

Should the radiographer deceive or mislead the patient when it is believed to be beneficial to the patient? It is an incontrovertible fact of law that all healthcare practitioners have an obligation to protect the patient from being subjected to harmful care. The code of ethics of every profession dictates a fiduciary duty to the patient also. This involves an accountability, that is, a public trust in giving healthcare services to society that assumes sound judgment be used in giving care competently.

VIGNETTE 16—EXPERIMENTAL RADIO-THERAPY

Mary Mottle was a widow, age 68, with a diagnosis of malignant melanoma. She was being treated at Quantum Medical Clinic with radiotherapy. The radiotherapy dose was experimental; it was used in animals but not yet in humans. Mary Mottle was given a year to live. She wanted to spend the remaining year with her daughter and grandchildren in another state. When Mary Mottle arrived at her daughter's, they began looking for a hospital or radiotherapy clinic to continue the experimental radiotherapy. No hospital was available for the experimental radiation dose treatments because none were convinced the radiation treatment was clinically sound.

It was suggested that Mary Mottle fly back to Quantum Medical Clinic for continued treatment and let Medicare pay for the expenses. On inquiring about the charges and expenses, Mary Mottle learned that Medicare would not pay for the transportation charges. Therefore, Mary Mottle would not be able to have treatment because she was unable to pay.

There has been some indication that the radiation treatments are helping Mary Mottle, because she is feeling much better.

What, if anything, should be done in this case for the patient or the experimenters of the radiotherapy treatment?

ANSWER

Mary Mottle's radiotherapy treatment is expensive and controversial. The prolongation of life is in doubt. There are only so many funds available, and there are others competing for the same funds.

Is this need a medical or sociopsychological one?

REVIEW QUESTIONS

1. Morality could be defined as:

   a. Statute.

   b. Fidelity to conscience.

   c. The good of society.

   d. Man-made rules.

2. A radiographer who would take the life of a terminally ill patient would be subject to:

   a. Negligence.

   b. Personally liable.

   c. Murder.

   d. Carelessness.

3. The following are ethical considerations for radiographers *except*:

   a. Conduct with dignity to the profession.

   b. Unbiased attitude toward race, creed, color, or nature of a health problem.

   c. Protect unethical conduct and illegal activities.

4. Ethical considerations are subject to philosophical, _____, and individual interpretations of what is right or wrong in a particular situation.

   a.   Psychological.

   b.   Legal.

   c.   Scientific.

   d.   Theological.

5. The radiologic technology code of ethics serves two major functions, regulation and

   a.   Education.

   b.   Morality.

   c.   Legality.

   d.   None of the above.

6. For the code to have regulative powers, the _____ will enforce the ethical codes.

   a.   ARRT.

   b.   ARRET.

   c.   CRT.

   d.   AMA.

CHAPTER EIGHT

PATIENT'S BILL OF RIGHTS

Upon completion of Chapter 8, the reader will be able to:

1. Recall the importance of the patient's bill of rights.

2. Interpret the patient's bill of rights published by the American Hospital Association.

It is a somewhat sad commentary on the health profession that a patient bill of rights must be committed to writing or to legislative enactments. Patient rights should be self-evident. The simple fact is that patients are entitled to dignity, consideration, and self-determination. Many state legislatures have passed a patient's bill of rights document either as a resolution or as statutory law. Some jurisdictions have limited the patient's bill of rights to nursing homes and others have extended it to include healthcare agencies. California statute states that it requires the patient's bill of rights be posted in all hospitals and medical centers. The healthcare facility exists to serve the patient. The patient did not come into being to serve as a hospital commodity or as teaching and research material for the healthcare system. Due to the complexity of the system and some of the reported abuses, it is necessary to inform patients of their rights while undergoing care. Patients should be made aware that they have the right to accept or reject treatments recommended by the physician or hospital staff, the right of privacy, the right to be free from unnecessary risk of injury, and the right to determine what is to be done to their body.

There is a consensus that the purpose of the patient's bill of rights was to reaffirm the concern of healthcare practitioners for the patient's human dignity. This reaffirmation is a new commitment to quality healthcare for all citizens and marks a new revolution for all healthcare consumers. The Constitution of the United States is a viable document and must be operative in all healthcare facilities for all patients.

A *right* has been defined as a claim to which man is entitled. A *right* by its nature is recognized by law and enforceable in a court of law. The following is the Patient's Bill of Rights published by the American Hospital Association.

1. *Considerate and Respectful Care.* The patient has the right to considerate and respectful care. Radiographers must be polite, display the appropriate respect, and be empathetic to the patient's needs.

2. *Complete and Current Information.* The patient has the right to obtain from his physician complete current information concerning the diagnosis, treatment, and prognosis in terms the patient can reasonably be expected to understand. When it is not medically advisable to give such information to the patient, the information should be made available to an appropriate person in his behalf. He has the right to know, by name, the physician responsible for coordinating his care. Radiographers must recognize the right of any patient who does not speak English to have access to an interpreter.

3. *Informed Consent.* The patient has the right to receive from his physician information necessary to give informed consent prior to the start of any procedure and/or treatment. Except in emergencies, information for informed consent should include, but not necessarily be limited to, the specific procedure and/or treatment, the medically significant risks involved, and the probable duration of incapacitation. Where medically significant alternatives for care or treatment exist, or when the patient requests information concerning medical alternatives, the patient has the right to such information.

The patient also has the right to know the name of persons responsible for the procedures and/or treatment.

4. *Right to Refuse Treatment.* The patient has the right to refuse treatment to the extent permitted by law and to be informed of the medical consequences of his action.

5. *Right to Privacy.* The patient has the right to every consideration of his privacy concerning his own medical care program. Case discussion, consultation, examination, and treatment are confidential and should be conducted discreetly. Those not directly involved in his care must have the permission of the patient to be present.

6. *Confidentiality.* The patient has the right to expect that all communications and records pertaining to his care should be treated as confidential.

7. *Reasonable Response to Requests.* The patient has the right to expect that within its capacity, a hospital must make reasonable response to the request of a patient for services. The hospital must provide evaluation, service, and/or referral as indicated by the urgency of the case. When medically permissible, a patient may be transferred to another facility only after he has received complete information and explanation concerning the needs for, and alternatives to, such a transfer. The institution to which the patient is to be transferred must first have accepted the patient for transfer.

8. *Conflict of Interest.* The patient has the right to obtain information as to any relationship of his hospital to other healthcare and education institutions insofar as his care is concerned. The patient has the right to obtain information as to the existence of any professional relationships among individuals, by name, who are treating him.

9. *Human Experimentation.* The patient has the right to be advised if the hospital proposes to perform human experimentation affecting his care or treatment. The patient has the right to refuse to participate in such research projects.

10. *Continuity of Care.* The patient has the right to expect reasonable continuity of care. He has the right to know in advance what appointment times and physicians are available and where. The patient has the right to expect that the hospital will provide a mechanism whereby he is informed by his physician or a delegate of the physician of the patient's continuing healthcare requirements following discharge.

11. *Explanation of Bill.* The patient has the right to examine and receive an explanation of his bill regardless of the source of payment.

12. *Hospital Rules and Regulations.* The patient has the right to know what hospital rules and regulations apply to his conduct as a patient.

The patient's right to information does not place an obligation on the radiographer to provide any and all information that may be requested. Radiographers must be prepared to offer explanations of the radiographic procedures and to identify themselves and the radiologists. Questions regarding diagnosis, treatment, and other aspects of care must be referred to the patient's physician and/or the radiologist.

Additional contemporary ethical–legal issues that deal with the patient's rights are abortion, the right to die, child abuse, involuntary commitment, informed consent, confidentiality, and invasion of privacy. There are other issues, but these have become more controversial.

VIGNETTE 17—INVASION OF PRIVACY SITUATION

Opal Opaque was a 45-year-old diabetic patient of many years. She was scheduled for an upper gastrointestinal series at Dynamic View Medical Center. Fanny Phosphor was a radiography student assigned to assist the radiologist with Ms. Opaque's radiographic procedure. Fanny Phosphor reviewed Ms. Opaque's chart and felt she would be an interesting case to present at the weekly student conference and film critique. Fanny Phosphor consulted with her instructor, Ms. Betty Beam, R.T., who advised Fanny that Ms. Opaque's would be an appropriate case for the conference and film critique on the gastrointestinal system presently being studied.

Fanny Phosphor began to talk more with Opal Opaque and learned Ms. Opaque had an alcohol problem. Fanny also learned that Ms. Opaque's husband was unfaithful, and Opal knew he had a young lover. Ms. Opaque told Fanny Phosphor she believed these things kept her diabetic condition irregular. At no time did Fanny Phosphor reveal to Ms. Opaque that she would be the subject of a weekly conference.

Fanny Phosphor made an excellent presentation of the patient's case, including the film critique, at the conference. Fanny brought out the effect of the alcohol and fidelity problems on Ms. Opaque's condition because she believed the staff would have a better understanding of Ms. Opaque's radiographic diagnosis. Following the conference, Fanny was called to the phone, and she inadvertently left her notebook with Ms. Opaque's case presentation in the conference room. Fanny Phosphor got busy with other radiographic procedures and completely forgot about the notes.

The radiology receptionist entered the conference room and found the student's notebook. The receptionist noticed that the notebook had Ms. Opaque's name on it and returned it to Ms. Opaque's hospital room.

During visiting hours, Mr. Opaque happened to see the notebook and noticed that the name and room number on the notes were those of his wife. Mr. Opaque read Fanny Phosphor's notes regarding his wife's problems. He asked to see the supervising nurse. He demanded to know why his wife was used for a radiography conference without her knowledge or permission. He also wanted to know why the slanderous and libelous statements about unfaithfulness were made about him. Mr. Opaque told the nursing supervisor that he intended to sue Fanny Phosphor, the instructor Betty Beam, R.T., everyone present at the radiography conference, and the hospital for invasion of privacy and defamation of character.

What will be the legal outcome? Should Ms. Opaque have been informed of the conference? Was Ms. Opaque's privacy invaded?

ANSWER

All persons present at the radiography conference are involved in the care of the patient and have a legitimate interest in information relating to the patient. Another issue not easily resolved is whether the communications made to Fanny Phosphor, student radiographer, were confidential and never intended to be exposed to any other persons. If Opal Opaque had known such information would be repeated, she should probably not have disclosed it to Fanny Phosphor.

It is obvious that poor judgment was used by the healthcare personnel in this situation. It would not appear that a cause of action for invasion of privacy could be sustained by Ms. Opal Opaque since the conference audience consisted of healthcare personnel. Since the radiology receptionist did not read the information, there is no need to address whether she has a "legitimate interest" in the information.

It was Ms. Opal Opaque who gave the information about Mr. Opaque's infidelity to Fanny Phosphor, so the action would appear to be against the wife rather than the radiography student. More importantly, truth is a defense to slander.

Mr. Opaque would have to prove that the statements were untrue and that he was economically harmed by them.

VIGNETTE 18—RIGHT OF PRIVACY SITUATION

Emma Insulator, R.T., is a staff radiographer at Cavitation Medical Center, who has worked in the radiography department for two years. Recently, a new radiographer, Ronnie Rheostat, R.T., has been hired to work the 3–11 shift. Emma Insulator notices that Ronnie Rheostat talks to all of the patients, asking them many questions of a personal nature not related to the radiography procedure.

One day Emma Insulator and Ronnie Rheostat were assigned to the same lunch period. While on the way to the cafeteria, the two radiographers were on the elevator, and Ronnie Rheostat said that one of the patients, Silvia Sinewave, told her she had been living with a prominent surgeon who was on staff at Cavitation Medical Center and had an illegitimate child by him. Ronnie Rheostat continued, nonstop, relating incidents about Ms. Silvia Sinewave.

Emma Insulator was concerned about Ronnie Rheostat's monologue regarding Ms. Silvia Sinewave. There were other people on the elevator. Ronnie Rheostat seemed completely unaware of the other parties on the elevator.

What, if any, legal implications are involved in this set of circumstances?

ANSWER

Discussing a patient's case on elevators, in cafeterias, or other public areas is a breach of the fiduciary trust and right to confidentiality to which patients are entitled as part of the "due care" owed by the institution. It can also be an invasion of privacy. This right to privacy was interpreted by the U.S. Supreme Court to exist for every citizen as part of the constitutional rights and is, therefore, an inherent right. The First Amendment, which guarantees freedom of speech and religion, has been interpreted as protecting the citizen's right to privacy.

It is unethical and unprofessional conduct to discuss anything of a private or personal nature concerning a patient. This is one of the most abused areas in patient relations. In the past, there was segregation in most hospitals for hospital employees and visitors, and this physical separation prevented visitors overhearing employees' conversations. Today, most hospitals share all facilities, and more contact between hospital personnel and visitors results. If hospital personnel are not cognizant of their professional responsibilities not to reveal any information about the patients, they should know that the discussions that take place between the patient and the hospital personnel are considered confidential communications. Any access to the patient's records or other data would come under the same classification.

The patient, as in this case, has the right to be protected from any disclosure of information that would embarrass, stigmatize, or cause her to be held in less esteem. This is not the same as privileged communication.

Privileged communication has special protection under the law. It has traditionally been recognized to exist between an attorney and client, clergyman and church member, psychiatrist and patient. Where communication is privileged, the confidence entrusted in the course of the professional capacity cannot be revealed and has special immunities.

All professional associations, including the American Society of Radiologic Technologists, are governed by a code of ethics that addresses itself to the issue of not repeating or communicating any information relating to the patient without appropriate or justifiable reasons.

This is obviously necessary so patients may feel free to discuss their problems, their illnesses, and other personal matters, with the full assurance that nothing will be repeated. The law considers the unnecessary disclosure of confidential information improper. To discuss the patient's confidential information with a third party is a breach of confidence. It is an unlawful disclosure for which the patient may have a cause of action against the party revealing such information.

REVIEW QUESTIONS

1. What item in the patient's bill of rights says that a terminally ill patient can refuse treatment unless the patient is incompetent?

    a.   Considerate respectful care.

    b.   Right to refuse.

    c.   Conflict of interest.

    d.   Confidentiality.

2. The patient has the right to know if the hospital or clinical facility is owned by the physician.

    a.   Conflict of interest.

    b.   Right to privacy.

    c.   Reasonable response to request.

    d.   Continuity of care.

3. The hospital must make sure the patient understands the bill for payment.

    a.   Hospital rules and regulations.

    b.   Continuity of care.

    c.   Conflict of interest.

    d.   Explanation of bill.

4. The patient has the right to know the procedure, risks, and alternatives.

    a.   Right to refuse treatment.

    b.   Complete and current information.

    c.   Informed consent.

    d.   Considerate and respectful care.

5. The patient has the right to see medical records.

    a.   Hospital rules and regulations.

    b.   Continuity of care.

    c.   Confidentiality.

    d.   Complete and current information.

6. The hospital must give to the patient highly skilled professional care and must provide referral for request of service.

    a.   Reasonable response to request.

    b.   Considerate respectful care.

    c.   Complete and current information.

    d.   Continuity of care.

7. There is a moral obligation in giving the patient his/her diagnosis and treatment in terminology that he/she can understand.

a.   Informed consent.

b.   Reasonable response to request.

c.   Complete and current information.

d.   Confidentiality.

CHAPTER NINE

RADIOLOGY SERVICE
IN THE HOSPITAL

Upon completion of Chapter 9, the reader will be able to:

1. Appraise the importance of the Joint Commission on the Accreditation of Healthcare Organizations.

2. List required department policy and procedure manuals.

3. Relate the importance of the radiology request for service form.

4. List the functions of the medical record and/or the radiology report.

5. Identify the medicolegal use of radiographs.

6. Recall the policy of ownership of radiographs established by the American College of Radiology.

7. Relate the importance of retaining radiographic films and radiographic films used as evidence, and of marking films for identification.

THE JOINT COMMISSION ON THE ACCREDITATION OF HEALTHCARE ORGANIZATIONS

The purpose of the Joint Commission on the Accreditation of Healthcare Organizations (JCAHO) is threefold:

1. To establish standards.

2. To conduct surveys.

3. To award accreditation.

The commission serves as an evaluator and educator rather than as an inspector or judge. It acts as a consultant, helping to identify both strong and weak points, and provides guidelines to assist in correcting the weaknesses. The JCAHO has become a colloquium through which the healthcare providers and related human services can be effectively motivated toward higher levels of quality and care.

The JCAHO is not a federal or state regulatory agency. It is a private, nonprofit corporation whose purpose is CHAPTER voluntary accreditation. Accreditation is based on ideal and achievable standards. Standards are developed from a desire to improve the quality of a particular facet of healthcare services. Changes in state-of-the-art medical practices and equipment and government regulations precipitate the need to review, revise, and develop new JCAHO standards. Consumer demands for accountability and the rising costs in healthcare have become important concerns in the revision and development of standards.

The standards of the JCAHO recommend the following policies regarding radiology services:

1. The radiology services in the hospital/medical center be directed by a qualified radiologist who is recognized by the American Board of Radiology.

2. There shall be adequate numbers of technical staff to conduct radiology services.

3. There shall be sufficient space, equipment, and supplies for the performance of radiology services.

4. There shall be written policies and procedures governing radiology services.

In every hospital and/or medical center that is accredited by the JCAHO, the JCAHO recommends that the radiologist be an active member of the medical staff and be available on a full-time or part-time basis, depending on the size and complexity of the radiology services. The radiology department director and/or administrative technologist should establish an effective working relationship with the medical staff, the hospital administrator, and other department services. The radiologist shall provide authenticated reports of radiologic findings. A radiation physicist should be available as needed for consultation, radiation safety, and education purposes.

POLICIES AND PROCEDURES

It is the responsibility of the radiology department administrator to develop and approve all radiology department policies and procedures. When this responsibility is executed thoroughly, the radiology department should function in a smooth and organized manner. The following list of department policy manuals should be available in every radiology department:

1. Department policy and procedure manual.

2. Quality assessment and improvement manual.

3. Infection control manual.

4. Safety manual.

5. Hazardous waste policy and procedures.

6. Emergency preparedness manual/disaster plan.

7. Continuing education manual.

8. Administrative manual.

9. Human resources policies and procedures.

10. Job descriptions, purpose, mission, and organizational charts.

REQUESTING RADIOLOGIC SERVICE

Requests for radiographic examinations are referred to the department of radiology. Each request is reviewed by the radiologist prior to the examination. Completeness of information pertinent to the patient's condition is important. Patient preparation, infection control, and isolation information and detailed instructions on how to move or transport the patient should be indicated on the request form. It is the responsibility of the radiology department manager and the radiologist to see that these examinations are performed promptly and efficiently according to the radiation safety criteria and legal codes.

PROCEDURES MANUAL

Procedures manuals are designed to meet joint accreditation standards, state standards, and hospital codes. The procedures manual may cover subjects such as appropriate gowning of the patient, transportation of the patient, and precautions to be observed in the transportation of the very confused, ill/medicated, or feeble patient, and patients in isolation. In addition, sequencing of each radiographic procedure using contrast media is included. The description of each radiographic examination covered in the manual includes the details of the procedure as well as the preparation for the study.

VIGNETTE 19—REVIEW PATIENT HISTORY

It is the responsibility of the radiologist to review the medical records of all in-house patients prior to any diagnostic examination. The radiologist, Dr. Watt, and the radiologic technologist, Amy Ohms, were performing an upper gastrointestinal series on Mrs. Syncope. Dr. Watt instructed the patient, Mrs. Syncope, to step up onto the footboard of the x-ray table to begin the fluoroscopic part of the procedure. Both Dr. Watt and Amy Ohms failed to read the patient's chart, which stated that

Mrs. Syncope had fainting spells prior to being transported to the radiology department. Mrs. Syncope, upon stepping up onto the footboard, fainted and fell to the floor. Mrs. Syncope sustained a hip fracture that required surgical correction. This unnecessary surgery aggravated a preexisting vascular disorder, causing Mrs. Syncope to have a pulmonary embolism.

Who is legally liable for damages and why?

ANSWER

The radiologist, Dr. Watt, is liable for not being acquainted with the patient's medical history. The hospital is also held liable for failure of the nursing staff who is responsible for completing the x-ray request form to include the patient's medical condition prior to transportation to the radiology department. In addition, the radiographer, Amy Ohms, was negligent for failure to anticipate the possibility of the patient fainting during the examination. The possibility of any patient fainting during any type of radiographic examination is part of the radiographer's training, and this knowledge imposes a duty to the radiographer to guard against this event or any other harm to a patient.

RADIOLOGY REPORTS/MEDICAL RECORDS

The medical records of a patient are a written account of what has happened to the patient during a special time. What occurs can happen in a doctor's office, hospital, nursing home, health maintenance organization, or any place in which medical care is given. The medical record and/or the radiologic report serves many functions:

1. It is a source of accurate communication between health -professionals and other legitimate or appropriate persons or agencies.

2. It is an official confidential document and is the physical property of the hospital or doctor's office or agency.

3. It serves as a data base for planning individual care and providing clinical data.

4. It serves as an objective witness to certain events that occurred in a healthcare setting.

The medical record and/or radiology report is required to contain sufficient information to justify diagnosis, course of illness, management, and treatment. Radiology reports are exclusively diagnostic reports of radiographic examinations.

Many court cases have been won or lost on the information written in the medical record and/or radiographic report. If a person initiates care or performs a procedure on the basis of standing orders or routine, the person doing the procedure should be certain to identify the reasons for the decisions to implement a specific treatment. Radiology reports are written like an investigative report, presenting only facts and not conclusions. Legally, the medical record and/or radiology request or report is important in any malpractice suit; it can be subpoenaed and brought into court. It is essential that the patient's name be spelled correctly. An incorrect name could infer that improper attention was given to the patient. Correct patient identification is basic to conveying accurate information. The method of admission into the hospital and/or the radiology department is important (i.e., stretcher, wheelchair, or ambulance), as is the time the patient was sent to the radiology department and the time the patient was released from the radiology department. All pertinent clinical information must be written on the radiology request form.

MEDICOLEGAL USE OF RADIOGRAPHS

The radiologist is a consultant to the medical staff, giving them reports of diagnostic radiologic examinations and/or treatments. The radiologist must sign the radiologic reports, which then become an integral part of the patient's medical record.

Ownership of Radiographs

Radiographs from private x-ray labs are frequently given to the patient who delivers the radiographs to his/her attending physician. The patient retains ownership. Portable x-ray services work in this manner also. Dental radiographs made by the dentist are part of the dental record. In a private physician's office, the radiographs are the property of the physician and part of the medical record. Radiographs taken in a hospital, clinic, or emergency center are the property of the facility. The patients and their physicians are entitled to the report but not the radiographs.

Policy of Ownership

The American College of Radiology has adopted the following statement regarding ownership of radiographs for the guidance of hospitals and physicians.

1. Radiographs should be used for the best interest of the patient.

2. Radiographs are the legal property of the radiologist, physician, or hospital in which they were made.

3. It should be the policy of the radiologist to make the radiographs available to the attending physicians with a copy of the report.

4. If the referring physician or the patient, on behalf of the referring physician, wishes to take the films away from the office or hospital, it should be clearly understood that the films are "on loan" and must be returned.

5. If the patient dismisses the referring physician and goes to another physician, the radiographs and reports should be made available to the new physician.

6. If the referring physician, on being dismissed by the patient, objects to the radiographs being sent to the second physician, the radiologist/physician must send the radiographs/ reports in spite of the objection.

7. All films should be diagnostic and permanently marked, identified, and dated.

8. When medicolegal situations exist, the radiologist has the right to refuse to release the radiographs for his own protection, except when the radiographs/reports are subpoenaed by the court.

Retention of Radiographic Films

Radiographic films are used for statistical purposes, for illustration of scientific literature, for teaching, and for medicolegal use. Radiographic films should be filed in the department and after one year stored in storage vaults that can be made available for reference. Radiographic film should be kept for a minimum of seven years, or until a minor reaches adult age plus one to three years. For example, in any particular state where the age of majority is 18 and the statute of limitations for any tort action is three years, the minor would have until age 21 to sue.

Radiographic Films Used as Evidence

Radiographic films can be introduced in a court of law as evidence. They may be introduced by the physician who directed the taking of the radiographs, or the radiographer who took them may be present to identify the radiographic films.

Marking Films for Identification

Radiographic film is valueless as legal evidence unless there is competent proof of its identity. The patient's name and x-ray number, date, and place must be imprinted on the radiographic film. Right and left markers must be permanently developed on the radiograph.

SAMPLE CASE: RADIOLOGIST LIABLE FOR ERRORS

Two radiologists were liable to a patient for $50,000 in actual damages and $100,000 in punitive damages, a Missouri appellate court ruled.

The radiological group, which was a general partnership consisting of two radiologists, first x-rayed the patient in 1965 in connection with abdominal complaints. Thirty-two months later, the patient was referred to the same radiological group for x-rays in connection with a complaint of soreness in his ribs. A resident employed by the group reported a lytic lesion in the anterior end of the eleventh rib. The report, which was signed by one of the partners, suggested that the lesion was a malignant tumor that had spread from its original location.

The patient's family physician, who had referred the patient to the radiological group, decided that the rib lesion should be removed for biopsy. A thoracic surgeon performed the operation, but a pathologist found no lesion. Further radiographs disclosed that the lesion was in the tenth rib, not the eleventh. A second operation was performed, and the lesion was diagnosed as a benign nonmalignant tumor. Testimony showed that the lesion appeared on the 1965 radiographs and was unchanged in the 1967 radiographs.

In the patient's suit against the two radiologists, a jury returned a verdict for the patient for $50,000 in actual damages and $150,000 in punitive damages. The trial court then ordered a remittitur of $50,000 from the award of punitive damages, which the patient accepted under protest. The patient had also sued the resident but later dismissed him from the case.

On appeal by the physicians, the appellate court said that the question of negligence in failing to look at the 1965 radiographs in the patient's files and in incorrectly identifying the rib was properly submitted to the jury. "It is apparent from the fact that plaintiff's lawyer discovered the earlier lesion in examining the radiographs at the first trial that the discovery of the lesion required no extraordinary medical skill," the court said.

There was testimony by the surgeon that he would not have operated if he had known that the lesion had not grown in 32 months. The surgeon was also sued by the patient, but he settled during the trial.

Evidence that the patient had undergone two unnecessary operations supported the submission to the jury of the punitive damages claim, the court concluded (*Smith* v. *Courter*, 575 SW Second 199, Missouri Court of Appeals, May 1, 1978, rehearing denied, June 12, 1978; transfer denied, January 29, 1978, *The Citation*, 33(3), p. 26).

VIGNETTE 20—DEPARTMENT POLICY SITUATION/EMPLOYEE RELATIONS

At a particular hospital, work schedules were posted at least two months in advance. One particular evening, a staff radiographer was scheduled to work 3 P.M. to 11 P.M. He did not come to work, nor did he call in. This had happen once before. The following evening he came to work when he was scheduled to be off. The supervising radiographer asked the radiographer where he had been the previous evening. He said that he forgot he was supposed to work and came to work this evening to make up the time.

What, if any, are some legal risks involved?

ANSWER

The hospital/medical center has a duty to each and every patient admitted to its premises for care; it has an obligation to implement standards to assure quality care will be maintained. Implicit in this obligation is the right to develop and maintain policies, procedures, rules, and regulations that give information and guidance to employees who work in the institution.

However, employees have certain rights. The have the right to know the policy of the hospital and what is expected of them as an employee. They also have the right to know what, if anything, will happen if they fail to meet those expectations set out in the job description or in the policies and procedures of the hospital.

Employees who consistently fail to appear for work without notifying their superiors or giving an explanation for their unacceptable behavior are subject to disciplinary actions. The disciplinary actions should follow the policy of the hospital. Any procedural steps should be according to the policy of the hospital. The supervising radiographer should use clear and concise language in documenting what has taken place. Any conference or discussion with the employee should be included. If a future course of action has been decided between the supervising radiographer and the staff radiographer, that also should be included.

The employee should have the opportunity to read the memorandum made by the supervising radiographer and sign it, or a copy of the memorandum should be given to the employee, or both, depending on the hospital procedure.

The memorandum should state facts and what the supervising radiographer perceived through his/her sense to be a fact. Judgmental terms and conclusions should be scrupulously avoided. If the staff radiographer refuses to sign the document, this should be noted. A copy of the document should be sent to the appropriate administrative parties, including the human resource director.

REVIEW QUESTIONS

1. If an individual is found guilty in a criminal case, the defendant:

    a.   Will automatically forfeit his/her license.

    b.   Will be expected to pay assessed money damages.

    c.   Will be expected to pay a fine or serve a jail term.

    d.   All of the above.

2. Restraints may be applied against the patient's will in certain circumstances, such as:

    a.   On a nurse's order.

    b.   If a patient is injurious to him/herself of other patients.

    c.   If there is shortage of staff.

    d.   If the family has requested it.

3. An incident report form should be completed:

    a.   For any untoward accident involving a patient.

    b.   For every medication error.

    c.   Immediately and a copy placed with the patient's chart.

    d.   Immediately and a copy sent to the hospital attorney.

    e.   According to the agency's policy.

4. Medical records and charts are important and necessary documents for which of the following?

    a.   Communication between healthcare radiographers and hospital administrators.

    b.   Legal evidence as documentation of certain patient events.

    c.   Research and statistical information for various government agencies.

    d.   Medical audits and accreditation and licensing processes.

    e.   All of the above.

5. Medical records and charting should be:

    a.   Specific, concise, accurate, relevant.

    b.   Factual rather than opinionated.

    c.   Source oriented rather than problem oriented.

    d.   Recognized as diminishing in value in the age of computers.

6. A legal signature on a document such as a medical record should have:

    a.   Name only.

    b.   Name plus professional status.

    c.   Sufficient data to assure specific identification.

    d.   Variations according to shift and agency policy.

7. An unconscious patient is brought into the emergency room bleeding profusely. The informed consent should:

   a.   Be held unnecessary under the circumstances.

   b.   Be signed by the next of kin, i.e., parent, spouse, child.

   c.   Be signed by the hospital administrator under agency policy.

   d.   Be signed by the patient as soon as condition warrants it.

8. Objectivity in documentation is most easily attained by recording:

   a.   The facts as you perceive them through your senses.

   b.   What your co-workers state about the situation.

   c.   What the patient says about his/her condition.

   d.   What assumptions you make because of your past experiences with the patient.

9. An incident report should be:

   a.   Completed by the radiographer in charge of the area.

   b.   Completed promptly and only with factual information.

   c.   Completed with the minimum amount of information.

   d.   Completed only after contacting the supervisor in charge of the area for guidance.

10. Basic Good Samaritan Laws generally protect radiographers against liability:

   a.   When giving emergency care in the course of their employment.

   b.   When giving emergency care at the scene of an accident without remuneration.

   c.   Only if no harm is done to the individual receiving the emergency care.

   d.   All of the above.

CHAPTER TEN

LICENSURE, CERTIFICATION, AND CREDENTIALING

Upon completion of Chapter 10, the reader will be able to:

1. Define regulation, certification, licensure, and accreditation.

2. Identify the purpose of licensure.

3. Discuss the concerns of limited licensure.

4. Explain the purpose of certification and accreditation.

In 1981, the U.S. Congress passed into law the *Consumer-Patient Radiation Health and Safety Act,* Subtitle 1 of Public Law 97-35. The act mandates the Secretary of Health and Human Services to develop federal standards for:

1. The accreditation of educational programs that train radiologic personnel.

2. The credentialing of persons who perform radiologic procedures.

The standards were issued and in 1985 were published in the Department of Health and Human Services' section of the *Federal Register* entitled "Standards for the Accreditation of Educational Programs for the

Credentialing of Radiologic Personnel." These standards are consulted in all states including the District of Columbia, Puerto Rico, the Northern Mariana Islands, the Virgin Islands, Guam, American Samoa, and the Trust Territory of the Pacific Islands.

The federal standards were developed as a model to provide a basis for consistency among states and are intended to encourage states to adopt uniform accreditation and credentialing qualifications for radiologic personnel. The federal law will preserve the state's traditional role in the regulation of health professionals. Therefore, compliance with these standards is voluntary, There are no penalties to the states if the standards are ignored. However, one section of the act established that in the absence of state compliance within three years, the Secretary of Health and Human Services shall report to the Congress recommendations for legislative changes considered necessary to assure the state's compliance with this subtitle. Therefore, these standards were developed as a model for the states in educational accreditation and personnel credentialing. Monitoring the state's conformance to the act is also mandated.

The two major credentialing processes in radiography are certification and licensure. Definitions of credentialing terminology, including the methods of implementation, identified as either governmental or nongovernmental, are:

1. *Regulation.* The intervention of government to control or change the behavior of participants in the marketplace through specifications of rules for the participants.

2. *Certification.* The process by which a nongovernmental agency or organization grants recognition of competence to an individual who has met certain predetermined qualifications specified by that agency or organization. Certification is normally granted by national professional organizations. Certifying organizations customarily dictate education, training, and competency requirements for applicants and offer certificate holders the right to use special professional title designations.

3. *Licensure.* The process whereby an agency of government grants permission to an individual to engage in a given

occupation upon finding that the applicant has met predetermined qualifications and has attained the minimal degree
of competence necessary to ensure that public health, safety,
and welfare will be reasonably well protected. Licensure of
health professionals is controlled by the state governments.
Many professionals are licensed in some states but not in
others. Licensure statutes will vary considerably.

4. *Accreditation.* The process whereby a nongovernmental
agency or organization evaluates and recognizes an institution or specialized program of study that meets certain
established qualifications and educational standards, through
periodic evaluation.

5. *Credentialing.* The recognition of professional or technical
competence by the government, private professional groups,
and certifying organizations.

LICENSURE

Licensure is a process in which a government agency authorizes an
individual to engage in a given occupation and use a specific title. The
professional privileges are contingent on the individual meeting specific
predetermined qualifications, assuring that at least a minimum degree of
competence has been attained. Licensure is under the control of the state
government. Licensure will not guarantee excellence. However, it will
ensure, at least, a basic competency level in clinical practice.

States that do not license and regulate radiologic personnel do not
require certification of operators of ionizing radiation. Therefore, there
are x-ray operators who have less than adequate or no formal training or
education in radiologic science. In many states, it is perfectly lawful for
a secretary, receptionist, or medical assistant, none of whom have had
any formal education in the use of x-rays, including patient and operator
safety, to administer ionizing radiation.

The basic purpose of licensure is to try to decrease the harmful effects
of excessive and unnecessary amounts of radiation to which the public is
being exposed by untrained and incompetent operators of x-ray equipment. The harmful effects of diagnostic radiation do not affect an individual

acutely or within years, but over generations, decades, and even centuries. The harmful effects of radiation on hereditary genes are cumulative and irreversible as they are passed down from generation to generation. Although individual incidents of radiation-induced deformities or illness are not predictable, what is predictable is that there will be a statistical increase in the incidence of certain deleterious conditions related to an increase in the overall radiation exposure to the population.

State licensing of radiologic personnel has increased since 1981 despite government opposition. The American Society of Radiologic Technologists, the American College of Radiology, and the state-affiliated societies have been instrumental in working for state licensure legislation. The American Society of Radiologic Technologists and the American College of Radiology have joined to develop model legislation that is more effective than the federal version.

LIMITED LICENSURE

The primary concern with the concept of limited licensure has been the lack of training required to obtain employment in this capacity. The most common types of limited license or limited permit are for chest and extremities. However, other categories include skull, spine, abdomen, pelvis, gastrointestinal, genitourinary, torsoskeletal, podiatry, and chiropractic.

California has issued over 11,000 limited licenses/permits in categories such as chest, extremities, torsoskeletal, skull, gastrointestinal, genitourinary, leg-podiatric, dental, photofluorographic, and dermatology.

The limited licensee is typically employed by a nonradiologist. Someone with very little medical background is simply shown which exposure buttons to push. Having limited knowledge in radiation safety and radiographic skills, the poorly trained x-ray operator could place the patient at risk.

Many radiologists and radiographers perceive limited licensure as potentially dangerous. However, despite the major concerns and conflicting opinions, limited licenses are becoming acceptable. Two thirds of the state laws currently in effect have provisions for limited licensure categories of practice.

The American Registry of Radiologic Technologists currently contracts with a few states to administer examinations of a limited scope. The American Society of Radiologic Technologists has published a curriculum for limited license.

CERTIFICATION

There are two certifying organizations for radiographers: the American Registry of Radiologic Technologists (ARRT) and the American Registry of Clinical Radiologic Technologists (ARCRT). The ARRT certification standards are more widely accepted within the radiologic community.

The ARRT certifies individuals who have met prescribed educational requirements and who pass the ARRT examination. Graduation from an accredited educational program in radiography is required for a person to test for the ARRT. However, the ARRT will consider, individually, the eligibility of applicants who are not graduates of an accredited program but whose formal training and experience are equivalent.

The ARCRT grants certificates to individuals who meet a prescribed combination of both education and experience and who successfully complete the ARCRT examination. Applicants are required to complete an accredited 24-month radiographic program or complete an approved military program in radiography.

Beginning in 1978, the ARCRT offered a challenge examination for individuals who did not have formal education and training in radiography but were on-the-job trainees with an equivalent of five years of full-time clinical experience. Applicants who pass the challenge exam become eligible to test for the ARCRT certifying examination.

In July 1994, technologists from the ARCRT joined ranks with the ARRT. The ARRT Board thus accomplished one of its major goals—to create one certifying agency in the United States. The agreement between the two organizations allows a technologist from the ARCRT to be registered by the ARRT; however, ARRT will not award certification since he/she has been evaluated on a different requirement. Instead, the ARRT issues a certificate stating that the technologist had passed an examination administered by the ARCRT.

The pocket credential supplied each year to ARCRT technologists would indicate that they were registered in good standing with the ARRT, but would designate also that they had originally passed an examination administered by the ARCRT.

In the future, ARCRT technologists may become certified by the ARRT if they pass the ARRT registry examination. Both organizations believe the agreement can only better the profession. One certifying organization can establish a more consistent set of standards for the profession.

Currently, the ARRT has expanded and includes programs of examinations and certificates in nuclear medicine and radiation therapy technology, which are other disciplines in radiologic technology. The present ARRT-recognized abbreviations for the three specialties of registered radiologic technologists are:

1. R.T. (R)(ARRT)—registered radiographer.

2. R.T. (N)(ARRT)—registered nuclear medicine technologist.

3. R.T. (T)(ARRT)—registered radiation therapy technologist.

4. R.T. (M)(ARRT)—registered mammography technologist.

The most significant event of the ARRT having impact on all registered technologists was the ARRT Board's decision to implement additional requirements for registry renewal. To renew registrations, technologists must either accumulate 24 continuing education credits over a two-year period or pass an ARRT certification examination in a category other than the one they currently hold. Enforcement began in 1997, and the requirements must be satisfied in the two years before 1997.

Radiologic technology is unique among the healthcare professions. Hazardous radiation cannot be seen, felt, smelled, heard, tasted, or touched. The hazards and properties of ionizing radiation are so significant that special operator training is warranted.

Since ionizing radiation possesses inherent danger and is not subject to the five senses, the proper use of ionizing radiation is dependent on the knowledge and competency of the individual giving that radiation. More importantly, it is the x-ray operator who directly controls any and all radiation that is emitted by the equipment. Therefore, minimal competency requirements must be established for certification and licensure of radiologic personnel as mandated by the Consumer-Patient Radiation Health and Safety Act of 1981.

VIGNETTE 21—REFERENCES

Ms. Penny Parallax, administrator of radiology services at Mottle Regional Medical Center, has been requested to send references on radiography personnel as part of her overall job function. Recently, Ms. Parallax was asked to send information about Nancy Neutron, R.T., an evening staff radiographer. There was a substantial amount of negative information on Nancy Neutron in her file. Ms. Parallax had several interviews and counseling sessions over her five-year employment at Mottle Regional Medical Center.

Nancy Neutron, R.T., had been suspended from the medical center for irresponsible behavior, including coming on duty intoxicated. If Nancy Neutron had continued to work for Mottle Regional Medical Center, it seems inevitable that Nancy would have been asked to resign or would have been fired for incompetence.

Ms. Penny Parallax wants to do the honest and right thing in giving a reference. She wants to be fair to Nancy, and she wants to be fair to the potential employer. More specifically, Ms. Parallax fears that she may be the subject of a lawsuit for defamation of character if Nancy were to find out that information was given and the substance of that information.

What, if any, legal risk is involved for the radiology administrator or supervisor?

ANSWER

Qualified privilege is a recognized privilege in which the public interest in activities that presuppose frank communication on certain matters between persons who stand in particular relationships to each other outweighs the damage to individuals of good faith, but where defamatory statements are relevant to the interests of those employers involved. This means that when an employer or valid representative of the agency gives an employee an evaluation or reference, that report is considered to be privileged information. The essence of the issue before us is "fair comment." As long as an employer makes observations and comments in a professional manner, without malice or vindictiveness, there is not cause for action for defamation of character.

It is necessary in the workplace for references to be exchanged among employers. The references must be honest and objective. The persons giving the references should be factual and not characterize the employee's acts. This is sometimes difficult to do; however, one should try to refrain from drawing inferences or conclusions. Let the reader of the evaluation do that. There are times when opinions are asked and must be given. The opinions that are given should have a basis in fact. There is no need to fear being sued for defamation of character if one sticks to these simple guidelines or rules.

REVIEW QUESTIONS

1. The Consumer-Patient Radiation Health and Safety Act of 1981 was developed as a model to provide consistency among the states to adopt _____ qualifications for radiology personnel.

    a.   Licensure.

    b.   Certification.

    c.   Registration.

    d.   Credentialing.

2. The two major credentialing process, in radiography, are certification and:

    a.   Licensure.

    b.   Registration.

    c.   Credentialing.

    d.   Accreditation.

3. The intervention of government to control or change the behavior of participants in the marketplace is called:

    a.   Licensure.

    b.   Regulation.

    c.   Credentialing.

    d.   Accreditation.

4. The process by which a nongovernmental agency recognizes the competency of an individual is called:

    a.   Licensure.

    b.   Registration.

    c.   Certification.

    d.   Accreditation.

5. A nongovernmental agency evaluates and recognizes an institute or special program of study. This is called:

    a.   Licensure.

    b.   Registration.

    c.   Certification.

    d.   Accreditation.

CHAPTER ELEVEN

HEALTHCARE REFORM
AND MAMMOGRAPHY

Upon completion of Chapter 11, the reader will be able to:

1. Identify the five categories of ACR accreditation in mammography.

2. List the medical industry's responsibility to mammography quality control.

3. Recognize problems that are found in most breast imaging centers.

4. Discuss FDA requirements regarding mammography certification.

Healthcare reform is inevitable. In fact, it has been happening for some time. The fundamental changes are being created by those who actually provide healthcare services.

The single most important limitation in the production of high-quality images is the radiographer. The radiologist and the patient are limited by the image quality of the mammogram.

Establishing standards of performance is complicated. The American College of Radiology (ACR), the American Cancer Society (ACS), the American Registry of Radiologic Technologists, state radiologic health branches, Medicare, primary insurers, and local and state radiologic societies are all involved in mammography credentialing and accreditation.

In 1987, the ACR established an accreditation program for mammographers in the United States. The ACR is responsible for the Board certification process for both diagnostic and therapeutic radiologists. It is a powerful political action group. The ACR accreditation program for mammography offers a way for healthcare facilities to demonstrate quality, and it has set quality standards to ensure high-quality mammography at the lowest patient dose.

The five categories of the ACR accreditation process include:

1. Qualifications of the radiologist.

2. Qualifications of the radiographer.

3. Equipment standards with regard to dedicated mammography units and performance variables.

4. Processor information and maintenance.

5. Establishing protocols for patient care, patient reports, and a quality assurance program.

Facilities that meet all of the categories of accreditation are awarded a three-year certificate.

The accreditation process is voluntary. However, there are some states that have legislated mammography laws that encompass the accreditation standards of the ACR.

California passed mammography laws in 1991. Many states passed laws that regulate not only the equipment but include a quality assurance program, the radiographers, and to some degree, the radiologists.

The ACR is now implementing a national system of standards in mammography reporting and record keeping. These standards will require reporting the reading accuracy of all radiologists. This will be a major step in forcing radiologists to become more accountable.

An estimated 11,000 mammographic x-ray units have applied for accreditation. More importantly, nine states now have legislation pertaining to regulation of mammography. The ACR accreditation is increasingly being used for both government and insurance reimbursement.

It has become quite clear that the radiologist, medical physicist, and radiographer all have important roles regarding mammography quality control. The radiologist performing mammography must assume responsibility for the quality of the mammogram and for the implementation of an effective quality control program. The radiographic staff's commitment to high quality will definitely mirror that of the radiologist. The radiographic staff performing quality control tests must be certain that the radiologist understands the program and must be interested in the results. The radiologist should review the test data and results periodically and provide direction when problems are detected.

The manufacturers of x-ray equipment, film, intensifying screens, chemicals, and film processing equipment, including dealers who sell these products, have important roles in the management of mammographic quality assurance. Industries' responsibilities for quality control include:

1. Designing x-ray units, screen film combinations, processors, and chemicals with the goal of producing mammograms of high image quality at a reasonably low radiation dose.

2. Providing high-quality and consistent products that meet specifications.

3. Defining appropriate quality control test procedures and communicating these procedures to the users.

4. Supporting their products in use by assisting customers in establishing and following quality control programs.

5. Helping customers identify sources of quality control problems.

Therefore, each member of the mammography team—radiologist, medical physicist, radiographer, radiology administrator, and the industry—must be included in the mammography quality control equation. A weak link anywhere along the quality control chain can contribute to degradation of mammographic image quality.

A comprehensive and cross-functional approach to quality control will meet the challenge of achieving the highest quality image and lowest radiation dose that every patient deserves. The quality of mammographic imaging is ultimately produced by the radiographer, not the ACR, the state, the ACS, or the radiologist. Radiographers' attention to continuing education, detail, and attitude will make a critical difference in the detection of breast cancer.

SOME MAMMOGRAMS MAY BE FAULTY

Ten Orange County, California, mammography centers were closed for flaws and violations. Thousands of Orange County women who have had mammograms may have undetected breast cancer because their x-rays were done at poor-quality centers, county inspectors say. Of the 96 mammography centers inspected in Orange County during the past year for state certification, 10 had to be closed immediately, according to inspectors with the Radiologic Health Division of the Orange County Environmental Health Agency. Only 15 facilities passed inspection outright.

The other 71 centers were given "fix-it-tickets," notices to correct inadequacies or problems in their operations that were not as urgent but could result in false-negative or false-positive mammograms. For example, mammography centers must have manuals that specify what technologists should do when a machine malfunctions. Without the manual to consult, the technologist could continue to take mammograms with a machine that needs to be serviced. Those mammograms could be faulty.

The state crackdown on mammography centers has substantially decreased chances of getting a bad mammogram today, but "thousands of women could have inadequate older mammograms," according to county inspectors Jim Hartranft and Trudy Papson.

No one knows exactly how many women have had substandard mammographies, and it is difficult for consumers to gauge the quality of their scans short of taking their films to an independent, certified center for a second opinion.

The scope of the problem is put in perspective by breast-cancer surgeons and radiologists who say they frequently see women whose breast cancers went undiagnosed for a year or more because of poor mammography. "At least once a week we see a woman whose prior mammograms indicated she should have been worked up at least a year earlier, and about half of those cases turn out to be cancer," said Doctor John West, a surgeon with the Breast Center in the city of Orange, California.

Violation notices issued by the state of California can be a good indication of a center's quality, but they sometimes present an incomplete or false picture, said Marie Dufour, administrator for the Marina Breast Center in Huntington Beach, California. The center was closed in August by county inspectors, who, working on behalf of the state's certification program, found the center's mammography machine had a broken automatic timer that was releasing excessive radiation. They also found poor film quality because of problems with the center's film developer.

The Marina Center fixed the problems, and it was reopened in September. The center's x-ray director said the staff did not use the film developer when it was broken and was working with the manufacturer to fix it when the county spot inspection was conducted.

"I thoroughly agree that there are some facilities out there that don' do quality mammograms, and I'm appalled just as any woman and any health facility should be," Dufour said. "We run quality checks every single day. We got closed for something so incredibly small that I can' believe they closed us down....They're so tough that they'll close you down for the smallest things." Other centers closed for quality problems declined to comment or did not return phone calls.

Dr. Jay Lichman, a radiologist with Hoag Memorial Hospital Presbyterian in Newport Beach, California, said, "Mammography is a very demanding technique. It is not like a chest x-ray where it is very hard to do a poor job. In mammography, everything has to be done just right. Any weak link in the chain can result in an unsatisfactory result."

On top of that, "It is very hard for a woman to judge for herself if she is getting a high quality study that is being interpreted by a well-trained physician." When a mammography center is cited for poor quality, it is up to the center's owner or radiologist to review old films for quality or errors. How many centers do that?

"Probably nobody," said Doctor Lawrence Bassett, chairman of the American College of Radiology's mammography committee and director of the Mammography Center at the University of California, Los Angeles. Dr. Bassett noted that mammography recommendations are based on the assumption that good quality mammograms are being taken.

Women ages 40 to 50 should have one every 12 to 24 months. Women 50 and older should have one every year. "Few women have mammograms as often as recommended, making it crucial that each mammogram taken is of good quality," the doctor said. A recent telephone survey of Orange County women by the University of California, Irvine, Cancer Surveillance Program of Orange County found that fewer than one-third of women 40 and older have the recommended number of mammograms.

"Some doctors have said that a bad mammogram is better than no mammogram at all. I think that is absolutely false," said Doctor Kathleen A. Ryan, Director of Mammography at Saddleback Breast Center of Laguna Hills, California. "A woman has no way of knowing if she has had a good mammogram, and she could get a false sense of security."

"Often women are looking for assurance that everything is fine," doctors said. They don't want to be skeptical about good news. If women learn nothing else, they need to realize that "a negative mammogram means nothing if you feel a lump. A negative mammogram does not mean you are OK," said Doctor Linda Southerland, a radiologist with Moran, Rowen, and Dorsey in Orange County, which specializes in mammography.

"I just saw a lady who has had a palpable (feelable) lump in her breast for two years. She saw on one of her reports that it looked like it could be benign cystic fibrocystic disease, so she never went back to the surgeon for a biopsy. She is a registered nurse and should have known better. When you see cases like this, you know it is total denial. I asked her why she finally came in, and she said, 'My husband made me come in.'"

Ryan says that one way to evaluate mammograms is to obtain a second reading from a center certified by the state and the American

College of Radiology. Nearly all hospital-based mammography centers meet both requirements and will do a second opinion, sometimes for as little as $25.

"While poor mammography can result in missed cancers, it can also result in more women being referred for evaluation who don't need it," West said. "We don't have a report-card system where people can find out if they are over-reading or under-reading. That means we could be missing a lot of cancers while at the same time putting a lot of women through the emotional trauma of a biopsy needle."

West explained that of a group of 100 mammograms, an accurate radiologist reading films might refer 10 women for more evaluation. Two of those women might have a biopsy, but only one would be breast cancer.

Common problems found by county inspectors at centers they ordered closed included:

1. Poor processing of mammography films. Old or improperly mixed and maintained developing chemicals resulted in unreadable mammograms.

2. Failure to use a licensed radiographer. Radiographers are trained in mammography techniques. Radiologic Technicians are limited permittees who do not have enough training to take a proper mammogram and are not allowed to take them. The use of unqualified technicians, including doctors, is illegal.

3. Equipment failures. Mammography machines are automated and have sensors to gauge the exact dose needed to obtain a clear mammogram, but in some instances, these sensors are broken.

Under the state's new system, women should see a certificate bearing the state seal on the mammography machine. Another indicator is an accreditation certificate from the American College of Radiology, which should be posted in the waiting room. The ACR accreditation, however, is done on paper; the mammography center answers written questions and sends samples of its mammograms for rating.[1]

THE FEDERAL FOOD AND DRUG ADMINISTRATION REQUIREMENTS

The Food and Drug Administration has indicated, as of June 1995, that radiographers who are performing mammography either hold the American Registry of Radiologic Technologists credential in mammography or have at least 40 hours of continuing education in mammography. More importantly, radiographers who wish to perform mammography but are not R.T.(R)(M)s must have completed 100 exams under the supervision of a "qualified" radiographer. "Qualified" refers to a radiographer who is either certified in mammography or has satisfied the experience and continuing education alternatives. According to the FDA, in healthcare centers that provide mammography, the following requirements must apply to personnel involved in any aspect of mammography, including the production, processing, and interpretation of mammograms and related quality assurance activities:

1. Interpreting physicians shall meet the following requirements:

    a. Be licensed to practice medicine in the state or facility in which they are practicing and be certified by one of the bodies approved by the FDA to certify interpreting physicians, or have had at least two months of documented full-time training in the interpretation of mammograms, including instruction in radiation physics, radiation effects, and radiation protection.

    b. Must have 40 hours of documented continuing medical education in mammography. Time spent in residency specifically devoted to mammography will be accepted if documented in writing by the radiologist.

    c. Must have read and interpreted the mammograms of at least 240 patients in the 6 months preceding application under the direct supervision of a fully qualified interpreting physician.

    d. Must continue to read and interpret mammograms from the examination of an average of 40 patients per month over 24 months and continue to participate in education programs, either by teaching or completing an average of at least five continuing medical education credits in mammography per year.

2. Radiologic Technologists shall meet the following requirements:

   a. Have a license to perform radiographic procedures in the state or facility where they are practicing.

   b. Have certification from one of the bodies approved by the FDA to certify radiologic technologists.

   c. Have undergone training specific to mammography, either through a training curriculum or special mammography courses, and accumulate at least an average of five continuing education units per year related to mammography.

   d. Have one year experience in the performance of mammography and by October, 1996 meet the training requirements specific to mammography, either through a training curriculum or special mammography course, and accumulate at least an average of five continuing education units per year related to mammography.

   e. Participate in formal continuing education programs and accumulate an average of at least five continuing education units in mammography per year.

3. Radiographic equipment designed for conventional radiographic procedures that have been modified or equipped with special attachments for mammography SHALL NOT be used for mammography. Radiographic equipment used for mammography shall:

   a. Be certified pursuant as meeting the applicable requirements at the date of manufacture.

b.   Be specifically designed for mammography.

c.   Incorporate a breast compression device.

d.   Have the provision for operating with a removable grid, except for xeromammographic systems.

4.   Quality assurance equipment shall be established and maintained in each facility to assure adequate performance of the radiographic equipment and other equipment and materials used in conjunction with such equipment sufficient to assure the reliability and clarity of its mammograms. The program shall also require periodic monitoring of the dose delivered by the facility's examination procedures to ensure that it does not exceed the limit. The average glandular dose delivered during a single craniocaudal view of an accepted phantom simulating a 4.5 centimeter thick, compressed breast consisting of 50 percent glandular and 50 percent adipose tissue shall not exceed 3.0 milliGray (0.3 Rad) per exposure for screen/film mammography and 4.0 milliGray (0.4 Rad) per examination for xeromammography procedures and be appropriate for the image receptor used.

5.   Phantom images shall be established and maintained in each facility to assess the performance of the mammographic system through the evaluation of radiographic images obtained with a phantom. The phantom must be of a type approved or accepted by the FDA. The phantom images must score at least the minimum required by the accrediting agency.

6.   Clinical images shall be maintained, and each facility will establish a clinical image quality control program which will include:

a.   Monitoring of mammograms repeated due to poor image quality.

b. Maintenance of records, analysis of results, and a description of any remedial action taken on the basis of such monitoring.

7. Surveys. As part of its overall quality assurance program, each facility shall have a medical physicist establish, monitor, and direct the procedures required for equipment, phantom images, and clinical images and perform a survey of the facility to assure that it meets the quality control and equipment standards specified by the FDA. Such surveys shall be performed at least annually, and reports of such surveys shall be prepared and transmitted to the accrediting agency. Each report shall be retained by the facility until such time as the next annual survey is satisfactorily completed.

Additional information regarding mammography standards can be found in *Mammography Quality Control: Radiologist's Manual, Radiologic Technologist's Manual, and Medical Physicist's Manual* prepared by the American College of Radiology, Committee on Quality Assurance in Mammography, 1891 Preston White Drive, Reston, Virginia 22091–5431.

The mammography certification offered by the American Registry of Radiologic Technologists remains voluntary. However, an increasing number of employers are requiring the R.T.(R)(M) credentials for staff and supervisory positions in the modality.

This trend, along with the preference for a multicompetent and multiskilled radiologic science professional, is likely to increase the burden placed on the radiographer, even without the ARRT's mandate for continuing education. A few years ago, the R.T.(R) qualification seemed enough for a lifelong career. Now, it may barely carry a radiographer through the first few years of employment.

ENDNOTE

1. Peterson, S. Some mammograms may be faulty. *The Orange County Register,* September 9, 1992.

REVIEW QUESTIONS

1. An accreditation process for mammography was established by the:

    a.   American Cancer Society.

    b.   American Registry of Radiologic Technologists.

    c.   American College of Radiology.

    d.   State radiologic health branch.

2. Support for mammography accreditation standards is increasing due to the increase in:

    a.   Breast lesions.

    b.   Malpractice cases.

    c.   Consumer awareness.

    d.   All of the above.

3. The record keeping standards that the ACR has implemented will force radiologists to become more:

    a.   Intelligent.

    b.   Accountable.

    c.   Aware.

    d.   None of the above.

4. The reviewer of quality control test data and provider of direction when problems are detected is the:

    a.   Radiographer.

    b.   Radiologist.

c.   Administrative radiographer.

d.   Hospital administrator.

5. The responsibility to provide high-quality and consistent mammograms which meet specifications is that of the:

a.   Radiologist.

b.   Hospital administrator.

c.   Industry manufacturer.

d.   Radiographer.

6. The quality of mammographic imaging is ultimately produced by the:

a.   Radiologist.

b.   Hospital administrator.

c.   Industry manufacturer.

d.   Radiographer.

CHAPTER TWELVE

FORENSIC RADIOLOGY

Upon completion of Chapter 12, the reader will be able to:

1. Understand the application of radiographic technique to determine cause of death.

2. Define battered child syndrome.

3. Identify signs of child abuse.

4. Discuss the legal implications toward child abuse.

The first forensic use of radiology in locating metallic objects in criminal cases was done in January 1896, four months after Wilhelm Roentgen discovered the x-ray.

A Mrs. Hartley of Nelson, England was shot in the head by her husband who then drowned himself in the Liverpool canal. He fired four shots into the head of his wife. Doctor William Little, General Practitioner, and Arthur Schuster, physics professor at Owens College in Manchester, tried to locate the bullets utilizing the newly discovered Roentgen Ray (x-ray).

The first exposure was noted as taking one hour in duration and the second exposure, seventy minutes. Dr. Schuster developed the bariumplatanocide plates and located three bullets inside the cranium of Mrs. Hartley.

The procedure that Dr. Schuster performed was using the Crooks' Tube. He brought three tubes to the house; he had two tubes as spares. He had a DC generator and glass photographic plates. There was no main electricity. The local company provided storage batteries to provide power.

According to documentation, one of the assistants to Dr. Schuster suffered a nervous breakdown attributed to the radiography of the mutilated and dying woman. It took a total of ten days to set up the apparatus and radiograph Mrs. Hartley. She died on May 9, 1896, fifteen days after receiving the gun shot wounds. This is documented in the "Nelson and Colne Express" which was the local newspaper (Knight & Evans, 1981, pp. 1–2).

The use of forensic radiology is to:

1. Determine whether bones are actually present, whether they are human, and to determine basic features such as age, sex, and stature.

2. Compare two sets of radiographs, ante-mortem vs. post-mortem views. A person's fingerprints are not the only parts of the anatomy that can be used for investigative purposes. Both dental and skeletal films are useful because no two people's teeth or skeletons are exactly alike. *Forensic dentistry* is the comparison of ante-mortem and post-mortem dental films. This is best known and widely used in forensic medicine. Almost everyone has had dental x-rays taken within the past five years, and the teeth are among the best preserved of the body parts, even in fire.

    Apart from the teeth and jaws, the most helpful part of the body for comparison radiography is the skull. The skull has more characteristic features, especially the paranasal sinuses. Other useful features are peculiarities of bony architecture and unique trabecular patterns. The cervical spine, vascular grooves, clavicle, lumbar spine, skeletal deformities, angulations, callus formation, congenital abnormalities, unique abnormalities, such as a dorsal defect of the patella, and the ossification patterns in the costal cartilage of the first rib are good areas for comparison.

3. Old injuries are a good way to identify bodies. An old chest film may be the only ante-mortem x-ray available on a John or Jane Doe. But in the upper corner of that film might be an old fracture of the clavicle that can be compared to the body in question. Foreign bodies, such as old bullets or shrapnel, are also helpful. Besides anatomical differences, prosthetics, synthetic joints, hip replacements, pacemakers, surgical implants, and disease processes make for easy identification.

DETERMINING CAUSE OF DEATH

Radiographic imaging techniques are also helpful in determining cause of death. Death caused by a penetrating wound, strangulation, drowning, electrical shock, metallic poison, and/or blast injuries can be easily determined radiographically. In multiple-injury cases, radiographs will enable the radiologists to discover which wound was fatal.

If a large caliber shotgun wound is made in the head, the skull fractures and there is massive brain trauma. When the bullet fractures across the venous sinuses on the inside of the skull, the sinuses are open to air. Negative pressure causes air to enter the vessels, travel down the jugular vein and carotid arteries, and finally enter the heart. Air entering the heart is probably why it stops beating.

IMAGING TECHNIQUES

Plain film radiography is the imaging technique most commonly employed by forensic radiologists for identification and/or discovering the cause of death. Other imaging modalities are used in special circumstances.

A fluoroscopic unit can be employed to recover foreign objects, such as needles and bullets, from bodies. Angiography is used to study vessel injuries. This is especially useful when investigating "surgical misadven-tures" and other iatrogenic problems. It is a law in San Francisco that all patients who die unexpectedly in hospitals must be examined by the coroner. All tubes and other equipment must be left in place. The bodies are studied for tube ruptures, catheter perforations, and other possible causes of death, often by an angiography.

Forensic angiographic techniques must be modified slightly when working on corpses because of the absence of blood circulation and washout. Positional and scout films are taken to define the region of interest. Since there is no washout, only one pass is possible, making it vital that the procedure be done properly.

A large load of contrast is delivered via pressure injector in one end of the vessels under examination and pumped out at the other end. Utilizing large amounts of contrast media will produce very clear and useful images. Most medical examiners and forensic radiologists use imaging equipment at county hospitals or employ the services of portable x-ray companies. If hospital facilities are used for forensic studies, the areas are disinfected after use.

There are two other x-ray methods that are used in forensic radiology, although they are not diagnostic techniques. Soft or low-energy x-ray studies using 10 kVp, 2 mA, can be made to find metal and bullet fragments, powder, and other particles on clothing and skin. This technique could not be achieved with clinical x-ray equipment because of its high energy output.

BATTERED CHILD SYNDROME

Radiology can play a vital role in the confirmation of the diagnosis of child abuse. Clinical examinations may reveal evidence of neglect, but a carefully conducted radiological exam can disclose not only the etiology of bone lesions but may give information on the approximate ages, number, and sites of bone abnormalities.

Battered child syndrome is defined as the radiologic appearance of bizarre and unusual injuries of the bones in affected children. These presumably result from repetitive trauma due to unawareness or deliberate denial on the part of those responsible. Radiographic evidence of the battered child syndrome, such as fractures of different ages in the same child, are accepted proof of abuse by the courts.

Perhaps the most telling sign of abuse is multiple skeletal injuries at different stages of healing. Classic radiographic findings indicating non-accidental injuries are epiphyseal and metaphyseal fractures. Injuries to the metaphysis and spiral and transverse fractures of the long bones may result from swinging the baby and/or forcefully wrenching or twisting the limbs.

Uncommon fracture sites, such as the lateral end of the clavicle, are usually encountered only following perinatal trauma or child abuse. Such an injury is probably produced by shaking or twisting. Sternal and scapular fractures are also suspect, as is thickening of the cortex and periosteal elevation. Rib fractures are also uncommon in childhood. Such fractures are frequently bilateral due to side-to-side pressure from adult hands grasping the child around the thorax and squeezing during shaking.

Brain trauma, subdural hematoma, and cerebral edema are the most common serious and urgent complications of nonaccidental skull injuries. This is often caused by whiplash from shaking the child. Radiography can provide supportive evidence for subdural hematoma by demonstrating separated cranial bones and widened sutures, other signs of increased intracranial pressure, or obvious fractures of the cranial bones.

Other suspicious head injuries include absence of hair or hemorrhaging beneath the scalp due to vigorous hair pulling, retinal hemorrhages, and jaw and nasal fractures. Abdominal injuries compose about 25 percent of the total injuries in child abuse. Injuries include duodenal and jejunal hematomas, rupture of the inferior vena cava, splenic rupture, renal rupture, gastric rupture, perforation of both intra- and extra-peritoneal organs, peritonitis, soft tissue edema, intramural hematomas of the alimentary tract, pancreatic injury, pancreatitis, and general bruising which can be documented by radiography.

Plain films of the abdomen reveal free gas or fluid in the peritoneal cavity or signs of peritonitis. Other radiographic evidence of visceral trauma includes pneumoperitoneum and/or ileus.

It must be remembered that suspicious injuries can be caused by other conditions. Some diseases also mimic abuse, such as scurvy, osteogenesis imperfecta, congenital syphilis, and infantile cortical hyperostosis.

The radiographer can gain useful information for the doctor by producing good quality radiographs for diagnostic interpretation. More importantly, the radiographer can gain the confidence of the child by being caring, honest, and friendly. In a friendly environment, the child may state the truth about how he/she was injured. The child may respond to questions better if he/she is not frightened when he/she enters the radiology department.

State laws require healthcare providers to report abuse to a child protection agency, such as the police or sheriff's department, county probation, or county welfare department. The *Child Abuse Reporting Law* specifically provides that neither the physician-patient privilege nor the psychotherapist-patient privilege applies to any information reported pursuant to this law. Not only is it considered a failure to report a criminal offense, but it is also a grave breach of professional responsibility to both the child and parent.

Hospital staff, including radiographers, should be familiar with the indicators of child abuse. Medical personnel should also be alert to "hospital shoppers." These are people who, for no apparent reason, have brought an injured child to a hospital outside of their community when their own community has fully equipped facilities. Often this is done to cover up a pattern of abuse since medical records sometimes reveal a history of hospital and doctor "shopping" that may, in conjunction with other indicators, be indicative of suspected abuse.

According to the law, specified medical personnel or their agents may take skeletal x-rays of a child, for purposes of diagnosing and determining the extent of possible child abuse, without consent of the parent or guardian. Medical professionals and other mandated reporters may be subject to civil damage suits if they fail to report.

SAMPLE CASE: *LANDEROS V. FLOOD*

In the case of *Landeros* v. *Flood* (1976) Cal. 3d 399, an infant, Gina, was brought into a hospital with injuries, treated, and released back to her mother. Subsequently, she was treated for new and more serious injuries by a second doctor who reported the injuries as suspected child abuse. The child was made a dependent of the court, and a guardian ad litem was appointed. The guardian ad litem then instituted a suit on behalf of the child against the first doctor for failure to report as required by law. The California Supreme Court reversed a lower court decision, which dismissed the complaint and held that the complaint stated a cause of action based on a failure to report as required by statute. The case held that failure to perform the statutorily imposed duty to report raises a presumption that a defendant doctor failed to exercise due care. The supreme court sent the case back to the lower court for trial. The plaintiffs in this case sued the doctor for $2 million, plus costs. A decision for the plaintiffs would obviously have been serious for the doctor involved. In spite of the ultimate outcome of this case (the charges could not be substantiated), it is clear that health practitioners and other healthcare providers who have a statutory duty to report may be held civilly as well as criminally liable when they fail to report suspected cases as required by law.

The importance of law enforcement's role in child abuse cases centers around the fact that child abuse is a crime, and that the primary consideration is for the protection of the child. Reports of suspected child abuse must be made to the police or sheriff's departments or other designated child protective agencies. Law enforcement personnel are also best trained to ensure protection of constitutional rights and due process procedures during the course of the investigation.

The responding officer will decide whether to take the child into temporary custody, to arrest the parents/caretakers, to seek the filing of criminal charges, or to refer the case to child welfare services or another appropriate agency. Final disposition should be made after consultation with representatives of other disciplines.

As in all other areas of criminal law, all searches, seizures, and arrests made in the course of child abuse investigations must comply with the requirements of the Fourth Amendment.

The National Center on Child Abuse estimates that between 2,000 and 5,000 children are fatally abused each year in the United States. These figures make it necessary that healthcare professionals, including radiographers, become more aware of abnormalities that may point toward child abuse.

APPENDIX A

SITUATIONS

VIGNETTE 22—INSURANCE SITUATION

You are a staff radiographer performing emergency procedures on "On Call Shift." Risk management data indicate that emergency "On Call" procedures is an area of high legal liability. You are concerned about your malpractice liability coverage. In discussing this issue with your radiology administrator, she states, "There is no need to worry—we have been told that all radiography staff are covered by the hospital insurance."

What, if any, are some legal risks involved?

ANSWER

Today we are all concerned about insurance. It is the civilized method of distributing risk. Most of us pay required premiums for health insurance, car insurance, life insurance, and home insurance. In fact, if one wanted—or could afford—to deal with Lloyds of London, one could have his hands or voice or any precious possessions insured for a sufficient premium.

Insurance is a contract or agreement by which an insurer agrees to assume certain risks of the insured for a premium. The insurer agrees to pay the insured, or certain persons, a specific amount of money if the event for which insurance has been taken occurs.

Insurance policies are usually elaborate, as most laymen know. In fact, lawyers, with tongue in cheek, advise that the best way of reviewing a policy is just to read the fine print. An insurance policy will contain the identification of the risk involved, the specified occurrence, and the specific amount payable should the event occur.

When analyzing an insurance policy, there are five distinct parts one should always review to have a better understanding of the actual coverage. The insurance agreement states what the insurer assumes to pay, or its legal liability, but not any moral obligations. There is the policy period which clearly states a certain period of time when the policy is to be effective. There is a defense and settlement clause which defines how the company will defend the insured against suit and its power to settle claims against the insured. The policy will have a clause stating the amount of money the insurer will pay, how it will pay it, and the maximum amounts it will pay. Finally, one of the most important sections of the policy is the conditions under which the policy will be paid. There are always important conditions in each liability contract, and failure to comply with those stated conditions could result in the policy being forfeited or cancelled. An insurance policy is a contract with legal obligations on both sides between the insured and the insurer. Failure to meet those conditions by either party is a breach of the contract.

By *risk*, one means that there is a possibility of some type of loss occurring. There are generally three categories of risk to which an individual is exposed. There is the risk to property, where one incurs loss or damage; there is the risk to person, such as injury to health or life; and there is risk to one's profession or legal liability, such as malpractice.

Insurance protection starts immediately when the agent gives the insured a binder. If no binder has been obtained from the agent, the insurance is generally not effective until the policy is delivered to the insured.

Obviously, it is difficult for the average person or family to bear the cost of serious damage to health, property, or person. Insurance is based on the principle that categories of persons exposed to the same type of risk or hazard pay premiums into a general fund from which the insured will be indemnified in the event the risk occurs.

The professional liability insurance policies give standard coverage using a clause such as "to pay on behalf of the insured all sums which the insured shall become legally obligated to pay as damages, because of injury arising out of malpractice, or error in rendering or failing to render radiographic services."

Do radiographers need to carry their own malpractice insurance? The answer, of course, depends on many factors that can only be judged by the individual radiographer who can weigh all the factors and make an intelligent decision. However, the author wishes to point out that few, if any, persons today would be without health insurance or automobile insurance. The risk involved in being without coverage is frightening to all of us. We are all aware of persons who did not have adequate coverage and whose financial resources were wiped out by lengthy illness. So, it would seem well worth the small premium for radiographers to carry professional liability insurance.

At present, the average malpractice insurance premium for radiographers costs about $50 per year. That seems a small price to pay for peace of mind. Another observation is that as long as one finds the premiums so low, it indicates that the lawsuits are not numerous. It is logical to assume that there is a direct relationship between the cost of premium and the risk involved.

Why do radiographers need individual liability insurance?

There is no assurance that a radiographer will not be sued individually even though covered or partially covered by the hospital or agency for whom one works. Also, even though the employer may be liable under the doctrine of respondeat superior for actions of the radiographer, the employer, through the insurance company, may file a claim against the radiographer to get back money paid out. This is called "subrogating the claim." The insurance company "stands in the shoes" of the employer. In fact, most insurance policies contain a subrogation clause which permits the insurance company to sue appropriate parties to regain any monies paid out under the insurance agreement. The radiographer can always be held liable for his/her own actions, whether named alone or as a co-defendant.

Malpractice liability insurance pays the court-awarded verdict and the cost of legal counsel. If you procure a $50,000/$150,000 policy, this means your insurance company will pay a maximum of $50,000 in damages to any one person injured as a result of your malpractice, and it will pay a maximum of $150,000 in damages in any one year on all claims against the radiographer.

Healthcare is a high-risk area for most of us. With advanced technology, educated patients, and increased risk of lawsuits, radiographers must be fully aware of what coverage they have and what coverage they need to be protected adequately in the event they must defend themselves in a lawsuit.

The malpractice risk for radiographers is significant, and recent indications are that the risks will increase in importance. Practically all persons involved in the radiographic field face the risk of a malpractice suit. A majority of radiographers recognize the significance of the risk exposure; those who have not done so should objectively examine their potential risk. The amount and limits of malpractice insurance should be commensurate with the risk of the radiographer, hospital, or health agency.

VIGNETTE 23—TEACHING ENVIRONMENT SITUATION

Mrs. Sally Solenoid is scheduled for a mammographic procedure. Doctor Angstrom, who is interpreting the mammographic films, decides to perform a breast examination on Ms. Solenoid. Prior to this examination, he asks three radiography students to observe the breast examination.

What, if any, are some legal risks involved?

ANSWER

There is often a misconception among health professionals that a patient who is admitted to a teaching hospital automatically becomes a subject for teaching, learning, and practicing procedures. This is not correct. Patients do not waive any rights, constitutional or otherwise, because they are treated in an institution which also educates radiographers. It is appropriate for the patient to be informed of who is attending her and under what conditions. All parties working with, and for, the patient should introduce and identify themselves by name and position to the patient. The patient always has the option of refusing the procedure, either the procedure itself or the person purporting to perform the procedure. The law is clear that admission of nonessential persons during procedures and treatments of a patient constitutes a violation of the right of privacy unless the patient has given consent.

Each of the parties, that is, Doctor Angstrom and the three radiography students, would be at legal risk for invading the patient's privacy if the breast examination is for the radiography students' benefit and not for the patient's benefit, and if the patient has not been consulted regarding the examination. The patient also has the right to be examined and treated by licensed, competent, and trained healthcare professionals. If less qualified persons are to be attending the patient, the patient should be made aware of this fact. It is then up to the patient to accept or reject the particular staff. Each time a patient is subjected to another unnecessary examination, it means added inconvenience and additional radiation exposure. Radiography students are learning and, therefore, presumably are not as academically competent and not as skilled at technique as licensed radiographers. We are living in an era of the consumer's right to know. Certainly, in the area of healthcare, the patient should be fully informed.

VIGNETTE 24—PROTECTING PERSONAL PROPERTY

Amy Ampere, R.T., is the evening radiography supervisor in a small community hospital. Ms. Marie Matter is admitted into the hospital complaining of vomiting and diarrhea. Ms. Matter has been admitted to the medical floor with a tentative diagnosis of food poisoning. On the way to her room, Ms. Matter is sent to the radiology department for a chest x-ray. Ms. Matter was transported to her bed after the completion of the chest x-ray.

While the nurse was taking her T.P.R. and blood pressure, Ms. Matter indicated that her diamond wedding ring which she had on her left hand was missing. Ms. Matter established that the ring is worth $500 and wants it back immediately, or she is going to sue the hospital for negligence in caring for her and her property.

Who, if anyone, is liable? What principles of law, if any, are involved? Is the hospital responsible for the patient's property? Would there be a different outcome if the patient were unconscious?

ANSWER

It is the general policy in most healthcare facilities to have available a place for safekeeping of any valuable articles. Upon admission, the patient should have been asked if she has any valuables that she would want placed in the hospital safe. If there are family present, the patient should be given the option of entrusting any valuables to the family. The hospital and the radiography personnel have an obligation to exercise reasonable care in protecting the patient's money and valuables. Reasonable care requires that the hospital provide a safe place and notify the patient of the opportunity to place valuables there.

The hospital or radiography personnel are not guarantors that the patient's possessions will not be stolen. They only promise to provide reasonable security. The patient was conscious when admitted and in control of her possessions. The patient has a duty to act as a reasonably prudent person at all times. It would seem the prudent thing to do is to take the precaution to notify the hospital personnel of the ring and the approximate value and request the article be placed in a safe.

When property is entrusted to the hospital for safekeeping, a bailment relationship takes place. Bailment is the delivering of personal property to another for a specific purpose. The bailor is the person who delivers the property. The bailee is the one to whom the property is delivered. When the purpose for the bailment is achieved, the bailee returns the article to the bailor. The bailee must take responsible care of the property entrusted and is liable for loss or damage to the property caused by the bailee's negligence.

The radiographer should make the necessary documentation and have a witness verify the specific amount, if money is involved, and the specific article, if rings, watches, or other valuable articles are involved.

If the patient is unconscious, the radiographer would have a higher duty to protect the patient's possessions. On admission to any unit, part of the admission procedure should be a protocol for covering the patient's belongings.

However, if articles are missing from the patient and the radiographer had no knowledge of the incident, neither the radiographer nor the hospital will be held liable. The standard of care is ordinary reasonable care, as long as the radiographer acts as a reasonably prudent radiographer would act in similar situations.

When patients are admitted to the hospital, they often bring several types of property with them. There is property having monetary value, such as money, rings, or watches. There is property of a personal nature, such as false teeth, eyeglasses, contact lenses, or other prostheses. There is property having religious or sentimental value, such as a Bible, medals, or crosses.

It is incumbent on the hospital and the hospital administrator to maintain an environment of safety and security for the patient and the patient's property. The law applied here is that of bailment. The patient has the right to expect that any property entrusted to the hospital's care through the agency of personnel working there will be returned intact. The hospital administration is not responsible for any property of which it had no knowledge. However, if any property which has been deposited for safekeeping is damaged or missing, the hospital would be liable.

There are certain precautions regarding property that reasonably prudent patients should take. Patients are bound by the reasonably-prudent-man doctrine. Therefore, the patient should not bring valuable property to a healthcare facility, since no healthcare facility can guarantee that nothing will happen to property in the complicated matrix system of a hospital. If the patient is admitted under circumstances in which he/she could not foresee or make preparations for the valuables on him/her, the valuables should be given to a spouse, or member of the family, with appropriate documentation of the event, such as a receipt from the family member.

VIGNETTE 25—SEARCH AND SEIZURE

Cathy Caliper, R.T., was working the 3:00–11:00 shift, and on a particular evening, a male patient, Benny Beam, was sent to the radiology department from the emergency room accompanied by two police officers. Cathy Caliper was ordered to perform multiple radiographs on Benny Beam. One of the police officers, Andy Anode, asked Cathy Caliper to search the clothes and belongings of Benny Beam while he was on the x-ray table during the radiographic procedure. The police officer, Andy Anode, wanted Cathy Caliper to locate any narcotics that were believed to be in Benny Beam's possession.

Cathy Caliper wanted to be cooperative with the police officer, but was not sure what legal risks were involved.

Should Cathy Caliper comply with the request to search for drugs patients may have in their possession? What, if any, legal liability could result?

ANSWER

The Fourth Amendment of the Constitution of the United States says: "the right of the people to be secure in their persons, houses, papers, and effects, against unreasonable searches and seizures shall not be violated, and no warrants shall issue, but upon probable cause, supported by oath or affirmation, and particularly describing the place to be searched, and the persons or things to be seized." The Constitution of the United States confers certain rights on all its citizens. The Fourth Amendment confers the right to be left alone, to be free from warrantless intrusions, to have privacy, to be secure in one's person and one's personal effects. This is not an absolute right but is a qualified right. This means the Fourth Amendment does not confer an absolute right of prohibiting all searches and seizures. It gives the protection of a qualified right and prohibits all unreasonable searches of a person or a person's personal effects.

In the landmark case of *Mapp* v. *Ohio*, 367 U.S. (1961), the Supreme Court ruled that any evidentiary material taken in an unreasonable search cannot be used against the person from whom it was improperly obtained in any court of law. This is called the "exclusionary rule of evidence" because such evidence is selectively excluded in a trial on the merits of the case involving such information or physical evidence.

The history of cases related to search have established that it is a fundamental rule that a search without a warrant is not reasonable unless an arrest is involved. If an individual is to be searched without a warrant, or without the individual consenting to the search, there must be an arrest. The general rule is that if the search precedes the arrest, and the search provides the basis or probable cause, the search would be ipso facto an unreasonable search.

The courts recognize the police officer's right to seize instruments, contraband, and the fruits of crime that are in plain view. This is referred to as the "plain view doctrine."

In the present case, one main issue is that the patient, Benny Beam, is not under arrest. If the patient were under arrest, Andy Anode would be justified in searching the arrestee, his clothing, and personal effects. These same articles could be subjected to laboratory conditions.

A warrant must describe the person, place, and things to be searched or seized with a reasonable degree of specificity. Exception to the general rule of requiring a warrant prior to searching an individual is where there are exigent circumstances and a clear indication that evidence exists, e.g., during a car accident, the arresting officer can search the individual and the immediate area but not the trunk of the car.

The patients, of course, could give expressed consent to search, effectively waiving their fundamental right of protection as guaranteed by the Fourth Amendment. This waiver would have to be completely voluntary and understood to be an intentional waiver of their constitutional right.

The Fourth Amendment does not protect abandoned property, but there is nothing abandoned in the present case. There is in the law the theory of custodial safety. In a 1960 federal court case, it was held that the law does not require return of property which could be used by a prisoner to harm himself or others. This case involved the protection of a prisoner and a prisoner's property (*Charles* v. *U.S.*, 278F. 2d 286 [1960]).

The conclusion to be drawn is that, as a general rule, the healthcare provider does not have the authority, the right, or the responsibility to search the patient. However, as with all, there is a common sense exception. It may happen that while caring for a patient, it comes to the attention of the healthcare provider that the patient has a weapon, such as a knife or gun, or a large amount of drugs. If reasonable healthcare providers would conclude from the known fact that the patient may harm others or himself/herself with the weapon or drugs, then the healthcare provider has a duty to act to protect the patient and other potential victims. The healthcare provider must take action as is commensurate with the imminent danger to the safety and well being of all persons involved. If the immediate danger calls for removal of the specific items, then they should be promptly removed. If the danger is not imminent or potentially dangerous, then the appropriate authorities, such as the administration, or legal authorities, such as the police, should be notified.

It is often general hospital policy that a patient admitted through the emergency room either conscious or unconscious will have his/her wallet removed for identification and safekeeping. Other items of value such as rings, clothing, etc. will either be given to the family members, if present, or placed for safekeeping by hospital personnel.

The key issue here is that this limited search is permissible in a medical emergency for the purpose of ascertaining identity. The primary role of the healthcare provider is to treat the patient and give medical care. The role is not to assist the police in their investigation nor to serve as an independent investigator. This is not to say the healthcare provider should inhibit, obstruct, or delay appropriate legal authorities while they are doing their job. But overzealous healthcare providers have been known to step out of their roles and act inappropriately and without authority. To search citizens not under arrest at the request of a police officer could place the radiographer or healthcare provider in the position of violating a patient's constitutional rights, by searching a patient's personal effects.

APPENDIX B

TRUE AND FALSE REVIEW: ANSWER KEYS

Determine which statement is true or false by marking **T** for a true statement or **F** for a false statement.

___ 1. Common law and judicial decisions are terms that can be used interchangeably.

___ 2. Statutory law and legislative enactments are terms that can be used interchangeably.

___ 3. Common law and legislative enactments are synonymous terms.

___ 4. An act committed by a radiographer involving assault and battery on a patient must be either a tort or a crime. It cannot meet both definitions simultaneously.

___ 5. Criminal law deals with conduct which offends society as a whole and not just the individual victim of the crime.

___ 6. Statutory law deals with conduct which offends one or more individuals in society.

175

___ 7. A radiographer who fails to act reasonably and prudently is considered to be negligent in the eyes of the law.

___ 8. The legal doctrine of respondeat superior applies to the acts of medical personnel only.

___ 9. The doctrine of corporate negligence states that the corporation has failed to follow established standards of conduct to which it is expected to conform.

___ 10. The doctrine of foreseeability holds that government and municipalities cannot be held liable for their employees.

___ 11. Generally, patients are expected to act as reasonably, prudent patients only under certain circumstances.

___ 12. A competent adult patient has the right to refuse radiographic procedures and treatments at any time.

___ 13. It is unnecessary to obtain an informed consent from an unconscious patient brought into the radiology department because the law presumes the patient wants to be treated.

___ 14. A radiographer who acts carefully and prudently cannot be deemed negligent for any of his/her professional radiographic activities.

___ 15. Malpractice refers to the negligence of a professional radiographer who has failed to meet the standard of care of radiographers.

ANSWERS TO REVIEW QUESTIONS

CHAPTER ONE
1. c
2. a
3. a
4. a
5. d
6. b
7. a
8. b
9. c
10. b

CHAPTER TWO
1. b
2. d
3. d
4. d
5. a
6. d
7. c

CHAPTER THREE
1. d
2. a
3. a
4. b
5. c
6. a
7. c
8. b

CHAPTER FOUR
1. d
2. b
3. d
4. d
5. a
6. b
7. c
8. c
9. b
10. a
11. c
12. a

CHAPTER FIVE
1. c
2. d
3. b
4. d
5. d

CHAPTER SIX
1. b
2. b
3. a
4. b
5. d
6. b

CHAPTER SEVEN
1. b
2. c
3. c
4. d
5. a
6. a

CHAPTER EIGHT
1. b
2. a
3. d
4. c
5. d
6. a
7. c

CHAPTER NINE
1. c
2. b
3. e
4. b
5. b
6. c
7. a
8. a
9. b
10. b

CHAPTER TEN
1. d
2. a
3. b
4. c
5. d

CHAPTER ELEVEN
1. c
2. b
3. c
4. b
5. a
6. a

ANSWERS TO TRUE/FALSE ITEMS

1.	T	9.	T
2.	T	10.	F
3.	F	11.	F
4.	F	12.	T
5.	T	13.	T
6.	F	14.	F
7.	T	15.	F
8.	F		

APPENDIX C

GLOSSARY

Absolute Right—Given to the person to whom it inheres the uncontrolled dominion over the object at all times and for all purposes.

Ad Litem—For purposes of litigation.

Administrative Law—Branch of law dealing with organs of government power and prescribes in the manner of their activity.

Affidavit—A declaration or statement of facts, made voluntarily, and confirmed by oath.

Age of Majority—Statutory or legal age of adulthood.

Agency—Includes every relation in which one person acts for or represents another by the latter's authority.

Agent—Person authorized by another to act for him.

Appeal—A complaint to a superior court to reverse or correct an injustice done or an alleged error committed by a lower court.

Appellate Court—That court in which judgements of trial courts are reviewed or appealed.

Arbitrary—Done without adequate determining principle, not done or acting according to reason.

Arbitrator—Neutral person chosen by both sides to decide disputed issues.

Assault—Threat to do bodily harm.

Authority—Legal power, control over, jurisdiction.

Battery—Committing bodily harm.

Binding Arbitration—Submission of disputed matters for final determination.

Borrowed Servant—An employee temporarily under the control of another. The traditional example is that of a nurse employed by a hospital who is "borrowed" by a surgeon in the operating room. The temporary employer of the borrowed servant will be held responsible for the act(s) of the borrowed servant under the doctrine of respondeat superior.

Breach of Contract—Unjustified failure to perform the terms of a contract as agreed upon or when performance is due.

Captain of the Ship Doctrine—Person in charge may be held responsible for all those under his supervision and makes the final decision.

Cause of Action—Averment of allegations or facts sufficient to cause defendant to respond to allegations.

Civil Law—Concerned with the legal rights and duties of private persons.

Civil Malpractice—Professional misconduct involving a criminal act.

Client—Person who retains or employs an attorney to represent him in legal proceedings.

Common Law—Derived from court decisions, judge-made law.

Comparative Negligence—Doctrine of negligence of the plaintiff and defendant is compared and an apportionment of damages is made based on the acts the parties are found to have committed.

Compensatory Damages—Amounts of money for proven loss.

Consent—A voluntary act by which one person agrees to allow someone else to do something. For hospital purposes, consent should be in writing, with an explanation of the procedures to be performed, so that proof of consent is easy.

Constitutional Law—Branch of law dealing with organizations and functions of government.

Contract—A promissory agreement between two or more parties that create, modify, or destroy a legal relation. It is a legally enforceable promise between two or more parties to do or not to do something.

Contributory Negligence—The act or omission amounting to want of ordinary care on the part of complaining party, which, concurring with defendant's negligence, is proximate cause of injury.

Corporate Negligence Doctrine—When the hospital as an entity is negligent. It is the failure of those entrusted with the task of providing the accommodations and facilities to carry out the purpose of the corporation and the failure to follow, in a given situation, the established standards of conduct to which the corporation should conform.

Crime—An action or offense against society as a whole.

Criminal Law—Deals with conduct offensive to society as a whole or to the state.

Cross-Examination—Examination of a witness upon his evidence given in chief, to test its truth or credibility.

Culpable—Blamable, censurable, connotes fault.

Death—Termination of life.

Defamation—Offense of injuring another's reputation by false and malicious statements.

Defendant—In a criminal case, the person accused of committing a crime. In a civil suit, the defendant is the party against whom suit is brought.

Deposition—An oral interrogation answering all manner of questions relating to the transaction at issue, given under and taken in writing before some judicial officer or attorney.

Due Care—That degree of care or concern that would or should be exercised by an ordinary person in the same situation.

Due Process—Certain procedural requirements to assure fairness.

Emancipated—The individual is no longer under the control of another.

Emergency—A threat to the life or health of an individual that is sudden and immediate.

Ethical Malpractice—Professional misconduct considered improper or immoral by the profession as a whole.

Ethics—The science relating to moral action or moral value.

Euthanasia—Easy and painless death.

Evidentiary Matter—Any species of proof or probative matter presented by the act of the parties for the purpose of inducing belief in the minds of the court or jury as to their contention.

False Imprisonment—Restraining another's freedom of movement without proper authority.

Fiduciary—Position of trust.

Foreseeability, Doctrine of—Individual is liable for all natural and proximate consequences of any negligent acts to another individual to whom a duty is owed.

Guardian Ad Litem—A guardian appointed to prosecute or defend a suit on behalf of a party incapacitated by infancy or otherwise.

Hearsay Evidence—Evidence not proceeding from the personal knowledge of the witness.

H.M.O.—Health Maintenance Organization.

Iatrogenesis—Produced inadvertently as a result of treatment by a physician for some other disorder.

Imputed—Ascribed vicariously to a person.

Indemnified—Made whole again, reimbursed.

Informed Consent—One in which the patient has received sufficient information concerning the healthcare proposed, its incumbent risks, and the acceptable alternatives.

Injunction—A court order to stop a party to the contract from performing the specific promise or act under other circumstances.

Invasion of Privacy—The right to be "left alone" to live in seclusion without being subjected to unwarranted or undesired publicity.

Jurisdiction—The court that has the authority to hear the case.

Law—The sum total of man-made rules and regulations by which society is governed in a formal and legally binding manner.

Legal—Permitted or authorized by law.

Liability—An obligation one has incurred or might incur through any act or failure to act, responsibility for conduct falling below a certain standard which is the causal connection of the plaintiff's injury.

Libel—Defamatory words that are printed, written, or published which affect the character or reputation of another in that it tends to hold him up to ridicule, contempt, shame, disgrace or to degrade him in the estimation of the community.

Litigation—A trial in court to determine legal issues and the rights and duties between the parties.

Lower Court (Inferior Court)—Court which has limited authority.

Malpractice—Professional misconduct, improper discharge of professional duties, or a failure to meet the standard of care by a professional which results in harm to another.

Mandate—Command or direction which is properly authorized and a person is bound to obey.

Medical Record—A written official documentary of what has happened to a particular patient during a specific period of time.

Mitigation—Abatement or diminution of penalty imposed by law.

Moral—Normatively human, what is expected of humans, that which they ought to do.

Mutual Assent—Clear understanding between or among parties considering an offer; known in law as a meeting of the minds.

Negligence—Failure to act as an ordinary prudent person, conduct contrary to that of a reasonable person under specific circumstances.

Nominal Damages—Token compensation where the plaintiff has proven his case but the actual injury or loss is not possible to prove.

Non Compos Mentis—Not of sound mind.

Offeree—One who accepts an offer.

Offeror—One who makes an offer.

Outrageous Conduct, Doctrine of—That conduct which is beyond all possible bounds of decency and is regarded as atrocious and utterly intolerable in a civilized community.

Parens Patriae—Duty of the state to protect its citizens.

Perpetrator—Person who commits a crime, or by whose agency the act occurs.

Plaintiff—The party who brings a civil suit seeking damages or other legal relief.

Policies—Guidelines within which employees or an institution must operate.

Power of Attorney—An instrument authorizing another to act as one's agent.

Precedent—A previous adjudged decision which serves as authority in a similar case.

Preponderance—Great weight of evidence, or evidence which is more credible and convincing to the mind.

Prima Facie—So far as can be judged from the first disclosure; on the first appearance. A prima facie case is presented when all necessary elements of a valid cause of action are alleged to exist. The actual existence of such facts is then subject to proof and defense at trial.

Privileged Communication—Statements made to one in a position of trust, usually an attorney, physician, or spouse. Because of the confidential nature of the information, the law protects it from being revealed, even in court.

Probate—Proving wills or handling estates.

Procedures—Mode of proceeding by which a legal right is enforced. A series of steps outlined by the institution to accomplish a specific objective or task.

Profession—The act of professing; collective body of persons in a profession.

Proximate Cause—Legal concept of cause and effect; the injury would not have occurred but for the particular cause; causal connection.

Punitive Damages—Money awarded as a penalty, damages relating to punishment.

Qualified Right—Gives the possessor a right for certain purposes or under certain circumstances only.

Quid Pro Quo—Something for something.

Reasonable Care—That degree of skill and knowledge customarily used by a competent health practitioner or student of similar education and experience in treating and caring for the sick and injured in the community in which the individual is practicing.

Reasonable Doubt—Ordinary or usual knowledge of facts of a character calculated to induce a doubt in the mind of an ordinary intelligent and prudent person.

Reasonably-Prudent-Man Doctrine—Requires a person of ordinary sense to use ordinary care and skill.

Rebuttal—Introduction of evidence to show statement of witness is not credible.

Redress—Satisfaction for the injury sustained.

Res Ipsa Loquitur—"The thing speaks for itself." A doctrine of law applicable to cases where the defendant had exclusive control of the thing which caused the harm and where the harm ordinarily could not have occurred without negligent conduct. Normally, the plaintiff must prove the defendant's liability, but when this doctrine is found to apply, the defendant must prove himself not responsible for the harm.

Respondeat—The person who argues against a petition or appeal, generally the person who prevailed in the lower court, the appellee.

Respondeat Superior—"Let the master answer." The employer is responsible for the legal consequences of the acts of the service or employee while he acts within the scope of his employment.

Right—Power, privilege, or faculty inherent in one person and incident upon another.

Rules and Regulations—Clear and concise statements mandating or prohibiting certain activity in an institution.

Sacrosanct—Not to be violated.

Sequester—Setting apart, to isolate witnesses.

Signatory—One who signs.

Slander—Speaking falsely about another with resulting injury to his reputation.

Standard of Care—Those acts performed or omitted that an ordinary prudent person in the defendant's position would have done or not done; a measure by which the defendant's conduct is compared to ascertain negligence.

Standard of Reasonableness—Measures how the average ordinary prudent individual is expected to act in certain circumstances.

Standards—Criteria of measurement and conformity to established practice.

Statute of Limitations—A legal limit on the time one has to file suit in civil matters, usually measured from the time of the wrong or from the time a reasonable man would have discovered the wrong.

Statutes—Legislative enactments; act of legislature declaring, commanding, or prohibiting something.

Statutory Law—Enacted by a legislative group.

Subpoena—A court order requiring one to come to court to give testimony; failure to appear results in punishment by the court.

Subpoena Duces Tecum—Bring the documents.

Suit—Court proceedings where one person seeks damages or other legal remedies from another. The term is not usually used in connection with criminal cases.

Superior Court—Court of the highest and most extensive jurisdiction.

Taft-Hartley Act—Enacted in 1947 by Congress, considered a pro-management law. It excluded nonprofit hospitals from federal coverage.

Tort—A legal or civil wrong committed by one person against person or property of another.

Unit of Employees—A group of two or more who share common employment interests and conditions.

Verdict—The formal declaration of the jury of its findings of fact, which is signed by the jury foreman and presented to the court.

Verdict of Acquittal—Argument that there is not sufficient evidence against the defendant to proceed and the case should be dismissed.

Viability—Capability of living, term to denote the power a newborn infant possesses to exist independently.

Vicarious—Substitute.

Void—Having no legal force.

Wagner Act—First National Labor Relations Act enacted in 1935 to protect workers' rights to organize and elect their own representatives.

Waived—Renounced or gave up a privilege.

Witnessing—One who testifies to what he has seen, heard, or otherwise observed.

Writ—A writing issuing from a court ordering a sheriff or other officer of the law or some other person to perform an action desired by the court or authorizing an action to be done.

BIBLIOGRAPHY

Akey, C. 1987a. Certification and licensure of radiologic technologists, Part I. *Radiologic Technology, 58*(6), 509–512.

———. 1987b. Certification and licensure of radiologic technologists, Part II. *Radiologic Technology, 59*(1), 55–63.

ARCRT R.T.'s to join ARRT R.T.'s in 1994. *Wavelength, 4*(12), 3, 1993.

Barber v. *St. Francis Cabrini Hospital, Inc.,* 345P Second 1307 (Louisiana Court of Appeals, May 13, 1977).

Berman, L., DeLacy, G., Twomey, E., Twomey, B., Welch, T., & Eban, R. 1985. Reducing errors in the accident department. *British Medical Journal, 290*(6466), 421–422.

Bouchard, E. 1992. *Radiology manager's handbook: The business of radiology.* Dubuque, IA: Shepherd Inc.

Buckleu v. *Grossbard,* 435A Second 1150 (New Jersey Su Court, October 14, 1981).

Bundy, A.L. 1988. *Radiology and the law.* Rockville, MD: Aspen Publishers, Inc.

California Administrative Code. Title 17, Part I, Chapter 5, Subchapter 4.5, 1969. *Laws relating to radiologic technology.* N.a.; n.p.

California Department of Fair Employment and Housing. Government Code, Section 7287.6 and 7291(f)(1) of the California Code of Regulations, Title 2, Division 4. *Sexual harassment.* N.a.; n.p.

Creighton, H. 1981. *Laws every nurse should know,* 4th ed. Chicago, IL: Year Book Medical Publishers.

Cushing, M. 1985. How a suit starts. *American Journal of Nursing, 85*(6), 655–656.

DeCann, R. 1985. What is a good radiographer? *Radiography, 51*(597), 127–132.

Doyle, E. 1991a. Morals in the workplace. *R.T. Image, 4*(46), 6–10.

———. 1991b. The fine line of the law. *RT Image, 4*(33), 3–6.

———. 1992. Is OSHA coming for you? *RT Image, 6*(11), 13–16.

Doyle, E., & Keefer, B. 1991. Sexual harassment: A hospital issue. *RT Image, 4*(12), 10–11.

Eckley, A.K. 1984. The role of radiology in forensic pathology. *Diagnostic Imaging, 6*(9), 145–159.

Ehrilck, R.A., & Givens, E. M. 1985. *Patient care in radiography.* St. Louis, MO: The C.V. Mosby Company.

Farwell v. *Boston W. R. Corporation,* 45 Massachusetts 49, 1942.

Gebhard, P.G. 1987. Securing informed consent: The radiologists responsibility. In A.E. James (Ed.), *Medical legal issues for radiologists* (p. 114). Chicago, IL: American College of Radiology.

Gerber, P.C. 1985. Good Samaritan laws. *Physicians Management, 25*(4), 99–100, 106–107, 111.

Graff, B. 1985. Anatomy of a malpractice trial. *American Journal of Nursing, 85*(6), 655–656.

Gurley, L.T., & Calloway, W.J. 1986. *Introduction to radiologic technology.* St. Louis, MO: Multimedia Publishing, Inc.

Hamer, M.M. 1987. Medical malpractice in diagnostic radiology. *Radiology, 164*(1), 263–266.

Hanson, J. 1989. Limited licensing: Why is the ARRT involved? *Radiologic Technology, 60*(2), 168–169.

Hatfield, S. 1992. Radiology helps identify victims of bizarre killings. *Advance for Radiologic Science Professionals, 5*(8), 5.

Hays v. *Shelby Memorial Hospital,* 546F, Su Court 259 (DC, Alabama, August 18, 1982).

Hemelt, M., & Mackert, M. 1982. *Dynamics of law in nursing and health care,* 2nd ed. Reston, VA: Preston Publishing Company.

Hospital Authority of Hall County v. *Adams,* 140 SE, Second 139 (Georgia, 1964).

Hunton, B. 1993. Good communication means good patient care. *Advance for Radiologic Science Professionals* 6(9), 9.

Keats, T. 1992. Manual labor and radiologic technology. *Applied Radiology, 21*(1), 13.

Keefer, B. 1992. Facing the risk. *RT Image, 6*(12), 12–14.

Knight, B., & Evans, K.T. 1981. *Forensic radiology.* Oxford, London: Blackwell Scientific Publishers.

Kramer, C. 1976. *Medical malpractice,* 4th ed. New York: Practicing Law Institute.

Kuntz, L. 1992. Piecing the past together. *R.T. Image, 5*(17), 41–43.

Leach, R.A. 1986. Technologist shortage? *Radiology Management, 8*(3), 55–56.

Malkin, L. 1992. Child abuse. *R.T. Image, 5*(16), 3–7.

Malpractice crisis: Public awareness by confused on details. 1985. *Medical World News,* 26(23), 21–22.

Mays, P.S. 1986. Organization and operation of the radiology department. In L.T. Gurley & W.S. Calloway (Eds.), *Introduction to radiologic technology,* 2nd ed. St. Louis, MO: The C.V. Mosby Company.

McCue, P. 1988. Update on state licensing of radiologic technologists. *Applied Radiology, 70*(2), 19–21.

Nelson v. *Patrick,* 293 SE, Second 829 (North Carolina Court of Appeals, August 3, 1982).

Partida v. *Park North General Hospital,* 592 SW Second 38 (Texas Court of Civil Appeals, November 15, 1979).

Peters, J.D. 1984. Malpractice in hospitals. *Law for Medical Health Care,* *12*(6), 254-259.

Peterson, S. 1992. Some mammograms may be faulty. *The Orange County Register, 10*(3), 45-50.

Pozgar, G.D. 1987. *Legal aspects of health care administration,* 3rd ed. Rockville, MD: Aspen Publishing, Inc.

Reitherman, R. 1992. The forces behind accreditation. *Radiologic Technology, 63*(3), 203-204.

———. 1993. Health care reform and mammography. *Radiologic Technology, 64*(5), 311-312.

Simpson v. *Sisters of Charity of Providence in Oregon,* 588 P Second 4 (Oregon Supreme Court, December 19, 1978).

Smith v. *Couter,* 575, SW Second 199 (Missouri Court of Appeals, May 1, 1978).

Spring, D.B., Tennehouse, D.J., Akin, S.R., & Margulis, A. 1988. Radiologists and informed consent lawsuits. *Radiology, 156*(1), 245-248.

The professional status of radiologic technologists. 1990. *Radiologic Technology, 60*(3), 246-255.

Tilke, B. 1995. FDA now requires RT(R)(M) or equivalent. *Advance for Radiologic Science Professional, 8*(18), 4.

United States Department of Labor. Employment Standards Administration. Wage and Hour Division, *Regulations,* Part 541, WH Publication 1281, revised June 1993.

Ward, J. 1985. Torts and technologists. *Educator: The Newsletter for Clinical and Staff Educators in Radiology, 11*(1), 1-2.

Warner, S. 1981. Risk management: An analysis of technologist's liability. *Radiologic Technology, 53*(6), 48-55.

INDEX